Find Peace on Purpose

The Intentional Transformation from Blaming to Being

Giulia Cappelli

Find Peace on Purpose

Giulia Cappelli

Published by Giulia Cappelli, 2024.

FIND PEACE ON PURPOSE

First edition. August 11, 2024.

Copyright © 2024 Giulia Cappelli.

ISBN: 979-8227235640

Written by Giulia Cappelli.

Table of Contents

Dedication

To the heart of the true shaman, all the healers and peace makers who Illuminate for the highest good of all concerned.

To my children, my three loves: My love for you began long before I knew your faces, personalities, voices; during the time when I could only sense your essence. My love continues while I have the honor to watch you unfold into exactly who you are. I am forever in gratitude to have carried you briefly on life's journey.

My parents, sisters and their families for their endless love and support. I know I have asked a lot and you have generously given so much.

Thank you, dad for the transformative banter. I miss you Always.

Mom, I am grateful for the times you cheered me on even when I fell silent. I appreciate your loving fire!

To Omak, the wolf of my heart, steadfast and radiant. A being with whom I felt completely in sync. I feel you are at my side. You were the one. I chose you and in doing so, I chose me.

To new love, my last love. The spiritual partnership that I have craved. The best is here and now and yet to come.

To the people in my life who see me and continue to track me as I change and grow, receiving what I offer in the way I intend. I would feel invisible without your reflection.

The University of Santa Monica (USM) and other organizations of similar vibration, for providing profoundly life changing education. USM took the puzzle pieces I intuited as far back as I can remember and offered me the construct through which I could bring the congruent bigger picture of my soul to Light. I am deeply grateful and honored to be a graduate. (UniversityofSantaMonica.edu)

And to my great nephew, who will likely be an amazing gift to science one day, who at the age of 5, when I was 55, asked me if I was going to have any more children. "How many eggs do you have left, Aunt G?", to which I smiled at the thought of this kid referring to my ovaries, and responded, "A few."

This book is one of them.

And so, may it inspire aliveness in you.

PREFACE

Peace on Purpose and the Wisdom Time Circle

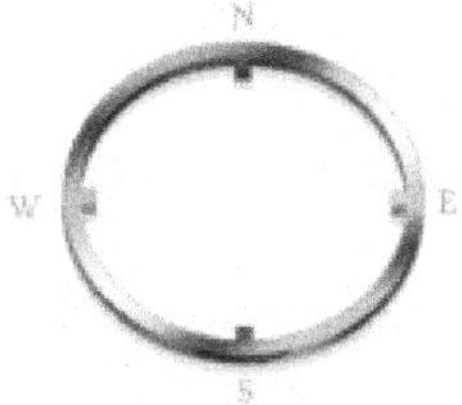

A little bit about me and how I discovered Peace on Purpose in my life.

I was born in New York City in 1966, the third daughter in an Italian American family. My grandparents emigrated to NY from Italy in the early 1900's bringing with them the cherished capacity for love from the hearts of my cousins in Italy. The first thirteen years of my life were lived in the Bronx, New York, where I made lifelong friends.

Subsequently, I moved to Westchester County, New York; graduated college in 1988 and got married in 1989, when I was working as a legal assistant. By 1996, living in Los Angeles, raising two of my three kids, I had a flexible job as a massage therapist, which is how I spent years learning to be quiet and listen to silence.

Motherhood revealed where the holes were in my emotional and mental development. In December 1996, I began a formal journey of self-discovery through Woman Within International, engaging in the retreat weekend and subsequent Empowerment Circles with women who changed my inner and outer world for the better Womanwithin.org

I sat with women in circle similarly to how our ancestors have for millennia. I received deep listening and began to get acquainted with the leader within me. It was time to start leading myself. It was during this time that nonsense began revealing its transformative qualities to me. The idea that being uncomfortable provided the B.S. I could use to fertilize a new way of thinking. I was taught to speak using "I" statements so to use language that conveyed that I was taking responsibility for my state of mind and heart.

Instead of "You hurt me when you didn't call!" I learned to say, "I felt hurt when I didn't get a call from you." This opened a new way of being for me and became the foundation for personal growth. As an aside. The first drafts of this book were written in the "I" viewpoint. My editor suggested the "we" perspective which I switched to though it goes against my natural inclination. I use the "we" form to embrace that I believe we are in this together. It is NOT my intention to speak "for" you directly.

Through Woman Within I learned about the spiritual psychology master's degree at the University of Santa Monica (USM). In 1998 I enrolled in the USM's Masters in Spiritual Psychology and extended the degree to include Counseling Psychology. (Universityofsantamonica.edu).

At the conclusion of year one, I was tasked with writing a paper explaining my own personal theory of counseling or consulting. I chose a circle compass approach, with human development life stages correlating to the four cardinal points, as a pathway to reclaim, reframe, reconcile and realign parts of my life. In May of 1999 I submitted my work, entitled "The Way of the Sacred Directions." This was the birth of what would later be called Peace on Purpose.

In September 2003, a week before my third child was born, I completed grad school. As the years and family demands progressed, I let go of the dream of becoming a licensed counselor. Support, finances and timing did not align in favor of it. Maybe I didn't push hard enough for me? It was an unfortunate decision, for sure. One that continues to fertilize my learning and inspire self-forgiveness.

Through the years I admonished myself for not finishing the internship to get licensed which actively created negative self-talk. I have said some very mean things to myself as a result. Not having that license limited my eligibility for employment. I have learned to forgive myself, trust the process and acknowledge how much I appreciate me, being me.

It had been my dream in grad school to one day have an organization that rescued dogs and worked with foster kids. In fall of 2010 I stumbled upon Wolf Connection Human Empowerment Programs. When I learned about the mission, I thought I had found my forever home to be of

service and I began to volunteer. I went from volunteer in 2011 to COO in 2017. After a few years I was leading programs and was confronted with the amazing opportunity to execute the Way of the Sacred Directions or rather the Peace on Purpose journey with group participants. Prior to that time, it was a coaching strategy I used on myself or shared privately.

For several years I actively role modeled Peace on Purpose, pointing out life's potential fertilizer to participants. I used conscious sharing and invited them to project their ideas onto my story by asking them questions about what they thought I felt or "should" say to my younger/older selves to promote taking responsibility and forgiveness. In the process they began to divulge their stories with ease, without pressure. Check out the empowering mission of Wolf Connection Wolfconnection.org.

I resigned from my position at Wolf Connection and departed in December 2019. I decided that instead of building someone else's dream, it was time to build my dreams, though my dreams were unknown at the time. I left what I had once loved so fiercely because I could no longer serve and be true to myself. I could not find a way to balance the job and have room for my unlimited expansion.

To have stayed would have been to consciously remain in a locked cage with the key in my pocket. To have stayed would have potentially limited an organization I loved because it was time for me to serve elsewhere. A good leader knows when it is time to move on; I hope that I respected the timing.

Wondering if I was brave and/or stupid, I walked away from my job in 2019 as I had done from my marriage in 2012. Leaving Wolf Connection was the second hardest painful experience of my life, and I am so happy that I dared to create and invite a new path. I advanced with some loving friendships and wolf ancestors firmly rooted in my bones, breath and voice.

I left knowing Wolf Connection's Program Director, now Executive Director, Dr. Amanda Beer, was continuing to cultivate the circle ritual with participants while training staff in the application of leading and witnessing. I imagine that the healing howl continues witnessed by good people through Dr. Beer's strength of heart, joy, supervision and of course the ever witnessing, wolves.

Me? I don't look back unless it's for Peace on Purpose.

Onward!

INTRODUCTION
Peace Starts with Me

Life brings many blessings and challenges. Love. Blame. Regrets. Gratitude. Some experiences can be very difficult to navigate with heart and compassion. To transform blaming to Being, we begin by embracing the regrets we may have and celebrate the learning with understanding and gratitude.

Along with gratitude and compassion, in response to challenges, who we "blame", and how we feel and think about ourselves, and others become the co-authors of our perspective. The perspective of the mind uses filters through which occurrences and people may be sorted into categories of "good" and "bad" throughout our lifetime until and unless we make new choices.

How to be is our choice in each moment. I try to increase my self-awareness and to cultivate peace. Finding peace is a striving for those who are willing to uncover and embrace potentially uncomfortable, poignant, and profound realizations to create connection. There is often a battle between the mind, that which has been scripted, and the heart which cultivates connection. Ideally, we continue to find inspiration and healing direction as we willingly explore with positive intention.

We can stop blaming others for the "bad" things that have happened to us and begin to sort through only those reactions over which we have some level of "control." As stated in the "Serenity Prayer" by Reinhold Niebuhr: "...grant me the serenity of mind to accept that which cannot be changed, courage to change that which can be changed, and the wisdom to know one from the other...."

Blaming takes so much energy because it goes against the natural flow of life. We may have become conditioned to think the natural flow is to blame self and others. I know that I was conditioned to blame others, and often myself, and to justify that. Blaming allows me to put myself in a superior position or an inferior position when I prefer to blame self. The natural flow is to take responsibility. I do admit that often I vent and complain before I accept full accountability.

As I began to take responsibility for me by releasing blame, I learned how to be me. A lighter, forgiving and more honest with myself, me. Let's review some typical exchanges between the "mind" and "connection" that our thought filters often encounter.

Separation and Connection:

<u>The mind says:</u> *These people are fools! I am better than they are.* Or *I hope I am better than they are.* <u>Connection asks:</u> "What's at risk if you were to discover you are the same as the "fools"? "What might you call the group then?" *I admit that I can be foolish. Maybe they are simply different from what I am used to.*

<u>The mind says:</u> *Not all my friends were invited to the VIP only party! I am good enough, better than Ted who didn't get the invitation!* Or *Am I good enough? Maybe I shouldn't go.* <u>Connection asks:</u> "What is at risk if you don't compare yourself to others? *Maybe we are all worthy of the invitation and there are only fifty tickets available. I am grateful to have the opportunity to attend!*

The mind says: I *found this wallet loaded with cash! Finders' keepers!* Connection asks: "Who is weeping for the loser?" *Instead of feeling superior, what are my options with respect to this wallet? If I keep this money, am I doing so with ill intention? Perhaps I can receive a financial reward from the owner who may or may not need the money more than I do. What is the best course of action for me and to show respect for the owner?* Connection asks: "What inner work can I do to see that maybe under the veil that shrouds my view of the world, there is only one wallet that belongs to all of us?"

The mind says: *What ridiculous beliefs they have in their religion! What I believe is the truth and only way.* Connection asks: "If you had grown up in that culture and religion, what would you have believed initially?" *These ideas are new for me. Hard for me to imagine and I can see that if I was conditioned differently, I would likely have thought accordingly. Maybe I am conditioned to be loyal to what I think, and someone is judging my beliefs as silly?* Connection asks: "What inner work can I do to assist identified solutions?"

The mind says: *That teacher is so amazing! I love the way they express themselves and make us laugh! I could teach that class with better results! Or I could never be anywhere near as wonderful as that.* Connection asks: "Do you know that what you see outside of yourself, also potentially exists within you? It is up to you to cultivate those wanted qualities to the best of your ability, authentically." *I wonder how my authentic expression will emerge. I believe I am capable of being an amazing teacher too. I am getting used to the idea. Or I never imagined that something so wonderful could be inside of me too.* And the part of self that proclaims they could do it better? "What is your intention in sharing such a statement?" "Is it about comparing your best to another's or simply seeking to grow yourself?" Connection asks: "Why the need to compare?"

<u>The mind says:</u> *What is wrong with parents today? Leaving their kids to spend hours using video games and internet technology!* <u>Connection asks:</u> "If we were to review generations, I wonder what other examples would be revealed of the things kids of a generation were left to do on their own." "Further, I wonder what similarities in familial legacies and economic backgrounds would be revealed." "Despite not appreciating the outcomes, can we have compassion for some of the reasons people do what they do?" "How many of them actually have ill intention?" "What might I be doing right now that someone else in the future may judge as selfish or neglectful?" <u>Connection asks:</u> "What can I do to be part of identified solutions?"

<u>The mind says:</u> *What happened to our old neighborhood? Nothing is the same! These horrible people who took over the block. They are not even from this country! It is such a shame!* <u>Connection asks:</u> "If we were to look back at when our families, potentially immigrants, moved into the neighborhood, how aligned do we feel with the sentiment towards specific groups at that time?" "How will the legacy of separation ever cease if we continue to look only to justify differences instead of embracing the many similarities?" "How will we see with our hearts that we are all people on a Time Circle journey?" <u>Connection asks:</u> "What inner work can we do to assist identified solutions?"

Peace starts with each of us. For me, the transformation from blaming to Being involves a therapeutic journey around a Wisdom Time Circle that is a circular "timeline" whereby we get to revisit our past, check in with our future selves and be more present in the Now. Basically, the things in life we have viewed as "shit" may be used as fertilizer if our "how to be" allows.

We look back briefly only to help us move forward in life. If we want to spend time investigating our past, we are encouraged to find a licensed mental health therapist. This Time Circle journey is to acknowledge and embrace who we have been, who we are now and who we are becoming as pertinent to our sacred timing for expansive personal growth and forward momentum.

As we move around the Time Circle, we explore our lives and welcome the opportunity to Reclaim, Reframe, Reconcile and Realign aspects of ourselves from past, present and in the future, embracing forgiveness and gratitude as we realign to a deeper truth.

- Reclaim is to pick up any lost pieces of self that may have been left in the past.
- Reframe is to infuse old belief systems with the truth.
- Reconcile is to bathe the experience in forgiveness.
- Realign is to mesh gratitude with the truth and clarity that forgiveness provides.

Finding peace does not mean that no one else should be accountable for their actions. It does not mean that we will suddenly want to spend time with people who have caused us pain. It means that as people, including ourselves, are held accountable, we "let it be." We are satisfied with accountability instead of choosing to unnecessarily add one more nail to their or our accountability "coffin", so to speak.

We all have seen or experienced that moment when another person or group accepts responsibility and asks for forgiveness. In that moment some of us may venture onto a pedestal to point a righteous finger, just because "they were wrong" and "we were right." Once we take a superior or inferior position, the path to true peace is compromised.

Peace on Purpose is a striving to maintain the possibility for humane centering even if it is never fully realized. We are human and advance in our own learning and timing. Let's be humane! We do our part to keep the path to peace open as we set healthy boundaries in place as needed.

Humane centering involves the following:

- The identifying, forgiving and release of painful self-talk, vitriol and blaming.
- Learning that the "good" and the "bad" that we see in others are also potential within each of us under some circumstance no matter how outlandish the circumstance might need to be.
- Understanding that in this crazy mix of life, we do not have to agree or like each other to be on the Peace on Purpose journey. It is possible to find peace, have healthy boundaries, and manage to co-exist.
- Identifying, revisiting and openly embracing the "Reality of Gratitude" in life. Gratitude flows more easily when the heart is open and continuously reaching for peace. We are grateful for many people and experiences that have enriched our lives.
- "Re-scripting" some of our former ways of thinking and being as we strive for deeper understanding of and take greater responsibility for our part.
- Choosing the option to touch the healing of aspects of ourselves we thought we left in the past.
- Being gentle with ourselves. This kind of work takes time and

we each have our own sacred timing to honor.

- Understanding that striving for peace means that sometimes we will still be mad and hurt. Hopefully we vent constructively. It is how we choose to be and what we do with the vented emotions and thoughts that determine if we are striving for peace.
- Being honest with and to the process. We might fool others, but if we are of healthy mental agency, we cannot fool ourselves forever.
- Knowing that when we center and heal ourselves in the microcosm, we also improve the macrocosm. Balance within and among all living systems is critical.

Healing invites connection. It is important to become aware of the thought processes we may be using in life on a regular basis and begin to expand our capacity for connection. It is easy to be separated from the people, things, and ideals that we judge as wrong or different in a "bad" way. Conversely, it is easier to feel connected to the people, ideals, and things we judge as "good."

Do we notice the separation that comes because of our judgements? Or when we feel judged hurtfully? Separation that may cause us to build a wall around our hearts instead of allowing a path of curiosity to exist between us and that which we view as badly different, negative, or wrong? Sometimes we also see ourselves as negatively different, or wrong.

With Peace on Purpose, I am inviting us to walk a path that I frequently amble along the Wisdom Time Circle comprised of points marking the four directions; north, south, east and west. Each direction represents a life stage.

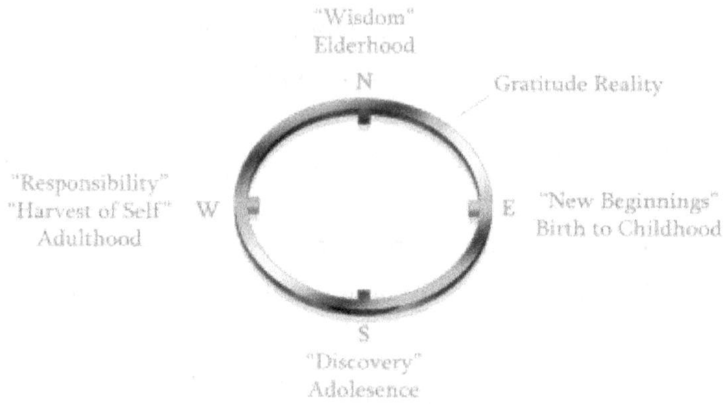

East is "New Beginnings" (birth and childhood).

South is "Discovery" (adolescence up to adulthood).

West is "Responsibility" (adulthood).

North is Wisdom of the elder who hopefully has Reclaimed, Reframed, Reconciled and Realigned sufficiently so to give back to younger generations.

The space from north to east is the viewpoint of Gratitude; where, ideally, we give thanks for all the lessons we learned as we look back on the journey. It is the domain of Morning Milestones: the regrets we gathered from mourning poignant milestones in our lives that in turn become our wisdom. Mourning to Morning Milestones become wisdom for a new day even if "time" is no longer on our side.

Let's read a snippet of Dana's Story for a brief overview of applying the Peace on Purpose approach.

Dana's Story around the Time Circle

Dana and Bill were pregnant with their first child and decided it was time to bring a dog into their home. As they prepared to start dog training classes, they unknowingly embarked on a revelation of their differences about behavior training. Bill was very straight forward in giving commands and in remaining rather even toned when reprimanding or instructing their dog. Bill was very matter of fact which to Dana seemed cold and void of emotion. Dana had come from a very passionately expressive family, that, she would later come to realize, had an emotional flair for the negative.

During dog training, Dana was instructed to praise the dog for successfully performing the request. She was asked to use an upbeat, sing song voice of accolade. Dana struggled to emit the sounds comfortably. In fact, she was acutely aware of how difficult it was to "praise" efficiently. What on earth was happening? Soon to be a new mother, and curious about her awareness, Dana explored and asked herself why something so simple would feel so very uncomfortable. Dana was surprised to find herself saying that she herself had not received a lot of praise growing up so, in turn, giving praise was not something that flowed for her.

Imagine the inner conversation Dana recently discovered around the Time Circle. Dana would find herself standing between the east and south of the Time Circle, finding the spot on the circle that represented a younger part of herself, somewhere between birth and adolescence, who perhaps was ignored or ridiculed instead of "praised."

Let's say that Dana pinpoints a memory to a time when she was around five years old and began to take it upon herself to set out the napkins and utensils on the dinner table each night. Instead of being praised, perhaps, often she was not acknowledged and instead told that something was missing or wrong with the set up. Because there were not important people in her young life role modeling "praising", it was as if that expression was not "learned". It didn't exist in her vocal muscle memory. Instead, as a child, Dana felt guilty that what she provided wasn't enough. Dana was more inclined to neglect praising others in her life and would often forget to express thanks because it was easier to point out what was wrong.

Dana practices and praises the dog in preparation to cheer on her child. Now that she has more awareness, in her sacred timing, Dana will take the Peace on Purpose journey and begin to praise that little girl who still lives inside of her. Later in life, Dana may visit her inner child and directly pay tribute to her, touching the pain and releasing more of the grief and guilt she had been carrying for over thirty years. The healing process, that began at the moment of awareness, continues when Dana speaks to her inner child using present tense and admits the poignant truth.

We can spend time talking "about" what happened to us and make some progress AND the real healing happens in the NOW which is why instead of speaking about what happened in the past we speak to those parts of ourselves in the present; because those parts of us still live in the NOW. We must meet ourselves where we are – at any age.

Dana, now forty years old, with an eight-year-old child, goes back to more fully heal the pain of her five-year-old inner self. Dana speaks TO her five-year-old inner child: *You are so great at setting the table without being asked! Such a helpful girl you are in the family.* As Dana expresses praise to her little self, she releases some tears: angry at feeling unappreciated, desperate for acknowledgement and sad that this happened to her.

She forgives herself for ever buying into the belief that she wasn't enough. The truth is that she is a darling and helpful girl. As Dana becomes more comfortable praising herself authentically, she, in turn, extends that authenticity to her child and out to others in her life.

Praise flows from her lips and becomes natural. So natural, in fact, that Dana discovers a flair for the positive.

Dana's story is a very common tale. There are so many people living life without following the curiosity of their own wisdom that will lead them around the Wisdom Time Circle of the Peace on Purpose journey. Dana could have chosen to stop with the awareness of what she was lacking in life and instead, she chose to heal more by actively inviting in more healing. She wanted to be better for herself and for her child. Blaming may limit the expanse of our love and expression of gratitude. As we heal the parts of ourselves that are hurting, we become more whole, step by step, and contribute to a better world because we will share that healing with others. Gratitude helps to heal our inner and outer worlds.

Here are some generic questions used to start the Time Circle journey followed by potential responses from Dana.

What's going on with me? *I am upset because I discovered that I wasn't taught how to give praise. I did not receive a lot of accolades growing up, so I am not comfortable giving praise either.*

Who/what do I want to blame? *I blame my parents. How could they be so cold?*

After Dana spews judgements about how others are wrong, what's at risk if her parents were right? In other words, what might Dana be trying to avoid believing to be true about herself? *I am avoiding facing that deep down I fear that I deserve to be ignored. My efforts do not deserve praise. My contributions are forgettable.*

Dana looks "in the mirror." *Have I treated others so harshly? Have I been neglectful? I don't want to believe that I have been cold to others too! How many people in my life have I not praised or thanked profusely?*

What was Dana forgiving? Rethink the statements of judgements and speak the forgiveness statement until she finds the combination of words that causes her to catch her breath with heart and emotion. Sometimes we do this in the spirit of "fake it until we make it" understanding that it might take time to get to the forgiveness.

I forgive myself for judging my parents as cold people who ignored a sweet child like me. Did they have malicious intent? I do not believe they hurt me purposefully.

Dig deeper if we choose: *I forgive myself for judging myself as unworthy of praise. As easily forgotten. As unimportant. I forgive myself for being ungrateful with others. I didn't realize how often I pointed out what was "wrong" instead of expressing gratitude. Like my parents, I did not have bad intentions.*

Then state the truth i.e., reframing the old beliefs and embracing the truth. *The truth is, I am worthy of being seen and heard and praised! In fact, each day I will look in the mirror and tell myself something wonderful like 'What a good job you are doing with ______.' I will also take time to express gratitude to at least one other person a day.* Dana makes a commitment to herself, to find a reason to share praise with herself every day. She knows that effort is self-loving and assists her in sharing kind words with others.

This is just the first brief example of how the journey works. This process will be presented in depth as we read more stories of others. At the very least, we will be inspired by the stories shared. Some of us may decide that the method presented does not resonate for us. If that happens, we honor the awareness!

To find and cultivate peace within us we are encouraged to use positive methods that resonate for each of us as we embrace productive inspiration to keep us moving forward. If we find ourselves struggling to move forward, we should seek further support from qualified professionals. If we find ourselves struggling text or call 988 for support (988lifeline.org)

Mindful Practice for Life Events

Note that instead of a chronological walk through the years of our lives to invite healing of aspects of self, the journey around the Time Circle can also be a mindful reflection regarding current life happenings. For example, as we start a new job we may stand at the east and consider the new beginning on which we are embarking. This is a way to explore and simply "check in." How are we doing in the south, Discovery phase of the new job?

Perhaps we are starting a new relationship. Feeling into that relationship, we can stand in the east, and consider its beginning stage. Consequently, we can walk the relationship through times of discovery, in the south. As the relationship matures, we can head to the west and consider the blessings of the partnership that are being harvested, taking responsibility for aspects of the relationship as is appropriate. It can be a wonderful way to check in with self, in the Now.

This attention to current life happenings may hone our intentions and expand our overall awareness and gratitude. The Time Circle does not discriminate. Where there is quality intention, there is a way.

Time Circle for All Ages

We are young and wonder how the Wisdom Time Circle applies to us? Consider that we, perhaps at age sixteen for example, can reconnect with the younger parts and we can also converse with our future selves!

If we have an inner child with unfinished business who suffered at the age of five, and we are now aged forty-three, we can use the Time Circle to go back to our inner five-year-old and have a healing interaction. It is never too late, or too early, for healing, no matter how many or few healing layers we may peel. Nor is it ever too late or too soon to visit, revisit or acknowledge gratitude for people and occurrences.

Moving Forward

We embrace gratitude for what we learn so we can do better and be better. There is a Gratitude Reality to most life happenings if we are curious enough to notice. We are curious when we are not so busy being right.

Mostly, on this journey, personally, I want to keep opening my heart. I want to keep forgiving myself and others until I am consumed with love. I know it sounds farfetched. Some people die trying. I want to live while doing exactly that; to be filled with love and forgiveness and ensure that the process has run through my heart, not just my "head" no matter how painful the release may be. When my head does the healing, the healing tends to be superficial and eventually dissolves back to where I started. The heart, however, keeps pulsing with the truth of transformation and anchors in the changes.

As we move forward, we will touch the pain, highlight the nonsense, the times in life that we judge to have been bad; where there is regret and blame, and/or point out the transforming gratitude.

We will face the truth about being honest with our willingness to embrace this process and defer to sacred timing as necessary.

We will follow some basic steps to fertilize old beliefs and grow new ones by exploring the Four R's: Reclaim, Reframe, Reconcile and Realign.

We will move forward regardless of whether this process is or is not familiar to us because we are curious.

We will listen to the story of others, and we are okay if we are not inclined to share our own story.

We will unpack our bags satisfactorily and carry on with levity and awareness.

We will allow ourselves to be inspired to strive for peace and try methods that resonate for us to give ourselves the best support.

Consider this: It is time for humans to revisit our true "humane nature" which in essence is the Peace on Purpose journey. How to be, to transform blaming to Being grateful and peaceful is our choice in every moment.

Together, let's start here.

Chapter 1
Considerations for the Journey

To offer you varying examples and perspectives as I continue to explain the Peace on Purpose process, I have organized the stories inviting you to dip into examples that involve my story along with the scenarios of fictional others. In Chapters Four and Five, I begin to share part of my personal journey with you.

In Chapter Three you are invited to experience the journey of someone named "Mike" so you can read through his process. In Chapter Two you will explore the "user manual" nitty gritty of a brief overview of human developmental stages, how to set up the Time Circle and how to use it with or without a witness. All the information is important to read through because when you are inviting healing, it is a sacred and precious journey. You, however, may choose to read it in a different sequence. Some people prefer to read the set-up procedures last because they require a deeper understanding before considering instructions.

Allow yourself to be inspired and trust your intuition as to the sequencing of chapters. Some of us may choose not to apply the experience to ourselves and instead will be open to receiving insight from the stories of others. We each bow to the sacred timing of our own healing journey.

The Peace on Purpose journey can be challenging because often many of us have not been conditioned to be humane with ourselves or others. Some perspectives may or may not be new for us while others may challenge our perceptions. I want us to feel supported in trying on new ideas. Do you know how in a fitting room, sometimes the mirror and lighting offer the worst reflection, and it can be difficult to "see" if the item looks good and fits well? I want us to be honest about what is being reflected. If it's a go, then "IT'S A GO!" because we view the whole congruent "outfit," we choose it and are ready to walk out into the world wearing it.

If it does not fit well (we individually do not choose it), it will calmly be removed and left in the fitting room as we continue to search for the right size and style. Sometimes, though we get inspired, we need to keep searching for the right fit. What is important is to keep going with the intention to seek peace. Sacred timing in this process is key.

The following sections share wisdom for our consideration. The intention is for us to open our awareness to the parts of ourselves that have been unfairly skewing our perspectives. We are becoming acquainted with new ways of seeing things and adjusting the filters we use to see ourselves and others.

I Am RIGHT

What is the most challenging aspect of the Peace on Purpose journey? I think once one opens to the concept, the most challenging aspect for many is walking the Time Circle, literally or figuratively, in the name of forgiveness. It is often easier to walk the Time Circle and point out the faults of others. To own my part as I walk the interconnected path? That may be more challenging.

I realize that some of us may struggle with this concept. I did! Like learning a new language, at first it may be easier to just go with it for a while. In learning a language what I suggest is that we accept that some nouns are masculine and others feminine, for example as in a romance language. Don't ask why initially because there may not be an answer or explanation that we will find acceptable. Basically, just try it out and move forward. Along the way, we find comfort in how it flows and discover ourselves speaking a new language.

To blame is easy! To forgive myself and others I allow myself to learn a new language and perspective. I do this to transform the heart of my perceptions. I am willing to see the Bridge of Curiosity in front of me. I am willing to try on this new experience and take the first few steps regardless of how I am feeling about proving that I am "right." There are times when our viewpoint in a situation may be correct. Having a correct answer does not justify building walls of separation.

I love many of Rumi's poems. This section of one poem speaks to the choice in "being right." *Out beyond ideas of wrongdoing and rightdoing, there is a field. I'll meet you there.* If we meet each other and ourselves in the field beyond judging and justifying right and wrong, perhaps we can connect.

As we drop the position of "we are right!", at the very least, maybe we will release some of the burdens we have been carrying and chalk it up to "there is more here for us to learn." This is a process: a path we will walk as many times as needed to allow forgiveness to pervade the heart. For some of us, being right is linked to our self-worth. Our hearts are worth more than that. It is possible to hold a correct answer and still live through the perspective of heart. The difference is that despite one party being "right," there is still connection instead of separation. For example, even though my position was "correct," I will apologize for the mean things I said to the other person. The stories presented in this book are shared to offer examples of the journey.

Crossing the Bridge of Curiosity

We see the bridge ahead of us and we are about to take our first step. We are standing on the side of what we have known to be true most of our lives, which is comprised of a combination of familial belief systems and being right seasoned with how we may be judging ourselves and others. We are willing to symbolically drop the bag of beliefs and righteousness to step onto the Bridge of Curiosity. We are willing to set aside the frustration or judgement we are carrying about what "just happened", so we have more room to explore. We can always turn back and pick up our bags at any time we may choose.

As we step onto the Bridge of Curiosity, we take a deep cleansing breath. We notice the potential lightness we feel in our bodies and the way we are walking now that we symbolically left our luggage at the threshold.

How do we feel in our bodies as we progress without a bundle of righteousness? What sensations do we notice? Honestly, some days my body feels heavy as I cross the bridge because though I left the baggage behind, however symbolically, the metaphor does not lighten my load. If that happens to us, it is okay. What great awareness we have since we noticed! Let's be gentle with ourselves.

Stopping at the center of the bridge we acknowledge self for the effort and willingness! We look around at the vista afforded to us from the Bridge of Curiosity. What do we see as we begin to shift the heart of our perceptions? We are being asked to let go of "being right". Know that we can return at any time, pick up our bags and continue if needed. Without carrying the load, we have more freedom to lean in a little with curiosity.

How to be in every moment is always our choice. I struggle with letting go of being right. I can be profoundly stubborn. My friends can tell you that about me. Here's how I talk to the part of me that resists letting go of "being right". When I get to the other side of the bridge, I ask that part of me to consider that in the end, I may still have the same opinion as to what I believe an answer to be.

The difference is that I will be more well versed in the position to which I am aligned. I likely will not want to or need to convince anyone else otherwise nor will I think others and their choices are better than or worth less than mine. I may find the need to acknowledge a healthy boundary with respect to whatever is happening. I can put up a "gate" to assist myself. This is a self-loving act.

The Bridge of Curiosity may expand our willingness to align with self without having to be "against" any other person or position. How does this sound?

We cannot predict the path of peace. Peace may come on a graceful wave that embraces All, it may come in purposeful increments, like healing and rehabilitating a broken bone and/or every variation in between. We do know that it is worth our efforts even if we find it illusive in its effects on the outside world. For now, we are focusing on our inner world.

Assessment Versus Judgement

Here are some considerations to help us deal with shifting the heart of perception from judging to assessing a situation. Transforming the heart of one's perception into being present involves recognizing the difference between judgement and assessment.

When we are in judgement, as I learned in my studies at the University of Santa Monica (USM) and Woman Within, Int'l, our soul's curriculum is being activated as evidenced by us going into emotional upset. It is okay to be upset. Being upset is often part of the situation. HOW we process and what we do with the 'upset', *how we choose to be,* determines how we may transform the heart of our perception.

If we do the work to Reframe, Reclaim, Reconcile, and Realign with the emotions and beliefs connected to the upset, then we are on our way to assessment and being present. Here is the thing, our conclusion or final decision regarding an issue may end up the same though the process and residual effects will be quite different.

For example, Pete is flipping out because suddenly his upcoming weekly schedule is packed full of meetings and due dates of deliverables. Pete is feeling overwhelmed, like he doesn't have time to breathe. I think many of us can relate to this scenario, yes? Let's take a quick look at judgement, assessment and how Pete gets to the conclusion for this scenario.

Judgement: Pete is angry. His new assistant should have seen that his schedule was getting overbooked. He is so tired of having to manage their every move! Pete's colleagues are too needy and could get by just fine with half the meetings scheduled. Pete must get his schedule under control!

Assessment: Pete realizes that his schedule got booked up and is unmanageable. He takes a deep breath and instead of blaming, he gives updated instructions to his assistant regarding how he wants his calendar to proceed and decides to accept 55% of the scheduled meetings presently on the calendar. He realizes that he could have given better instructions. He updates his assistant and sends a quick email off to HR to add information to the training for future assistants.

Moving forward he has a new plan to support his calendar in staying balanced with the amount of quiet work he wants and meetings required for him to be productive and focused.

The conclusion to get the current and ongoing schedule altered to be conducive to Pete being productive has been accomplished. By what means was this accomplished? When in anger, in the upset, Pete could have blamed others for the situation he was in. And yes – maybe his assistant made a mistake and overbooked his calendar. Life happens.

How one gets to the conclusion is just as important as the conclusion. When Pete takes responsibility, centers back to balance and devises a plan for the upcoming week and how to proceed with future meeting dates he "fixes" the problem and moves forward with clarity and little to no baggage. Pete is not angrily grabbing a coffee in the work kitchen while talking to himself about how dumb his assistant turned out to be.

Does the result justify the method used in response to the issue? At what cost? Some people might say that both choices were comparable. I think how Pete gets there is critical. One way he is blaming and dismantling professional relationships while the other way he is being responsible. Regardless, he manages to center himself and proceeds without dismantling relationships or jeopardizing work product and honoring his physiological health by reducing stress in his body.

There is a cost to acting under the blanket of the end justifies the means. How I am being as I get there is just as important as getting there. Clearly the means are important to maintain a positive and professional work environment. Additionally, the means are important to support Pete in taking responsibility for his reaction, design a balanced response and move forward.

The Bridge of Curiosity supports us in taking responsibility for upset. It is okay to be upset. We are human! What we do with upset is our choice. We can use it as fertilizer to positively transform whatever situation we are experiencing to the best of our ability, or we can choose to blame others or the situation.

When we blame others we consciously or unconsciously tell ourselves that we are better than or less than the others. Some people may do that to survive in life. We are not here to judge the why. We all have our stories of why we do and choose certain things. By facing our upset as soon as possible, we are noting what keeps us separate from self and others. Generally, fear and anger are the culprits.

Sometimes we may struggle with personal growth and blame others and circumstances. We are human and do vent sometimes in unproductive ways. However, we can take responsibility for our transgressions albeit before, during and/or after the episodes. We become conscious of our "mistakes" or rather what we are learning and are open to having others challenge us if we attempt to fool ourselves.

We reviewed an example of judgement versus assessment regarding Pete. Now let's look at a few strategies I like to use to stop me from separating myself from others. Strategies to assist me in being centered as I assess, to help me thwart my ego from rating others and myself as more than or less than and to maintain a heart centered perception.

Own the Connection

It is important to identify how we are being when we cultivate connection versus separation from self and others. Connection is born when we recognize that under some circumstances, no matter how outlandish those circumstances might need to be, we are just as capable of doing the "good" or "bad" things that we see in others.

Here's the thing, it may not be *probable* for us to commit murder AND it is *possible* under some circumstances. If we are willing to own the reflection of judgements we have of others, we begin to remove the separation that divides humans from each other and sometimes from balance with life itself.

The "Connection" lives on the Bridge of Curiosity. The connection is understanding that under some circumstances, even if those circumstances involved an alien invasion and hell freezing over, we are capable of the same. It's a bridge instead of a wall. The bridge is there to hold the space signifying that we are connected even though we are not all the same based on our choices and their outcomes.

Another example would be that it is not probable in this lifetime that I would vote against women's rights, and it is possible under some circumstances. Do you see how in me owning this example that I remain in connection to people who may live under that label of voting against women's rights? I am not above them or below them.

I do not HAVE to damn anyone, and I do not have to share leisurely meals with them or be besties. I can still support jailing those convicted, who in truth committed the crime, and agree or disagree with the choices of others without being "above" them as if I am some different type of human than they.

I know that there are people who on the surface may not even seem human; they commit gruesome crimes. I am not condoning that by stepping onto the Bridge of Curiosity. I get it. It would take an alien invasion plus a lot extra for most of us to make that kind of choice. What I am suggesting is that what we see in those times is an expression of the why of their story, likely infused with debilitating and dangerous mental illness.

I am not asking anyone to align with this. I am suggesting that somewhere above and/or under the horror, beauty, the mess or B.S. of the mix of life, there is a path of connection for which under some circumstances, we are all "capable." How we choose to be in every moment may be an entirely different story.

The impasses facing humans seem insurmountable and they may be in our lifetime. Imagine though that the wind is blowing and just maybe, if we each work on Peace on Purpose, the winds will move in a direction that assists us in creating a surmountable perspective. Join me on the tendril like breezes that flow through humanity. Together we can accomplish so much if we strive according to our own timing.

In the beginning and in the end, we are all capable of the same however improbable it may be that we would all agree on a course of action. If I am busy being right with the intention of saying how others are wrong along with how I would never and could never be like *that,* then I am using my life force to dismantle my bridge of connection to All starting with my connection to myself. This is a choice of how to be.

How secure is your bridge in this life? The state of this world has people at odds, maybe more so in recent years. I often wonder if we are more at odds because so much of what used to be in the shadow has been more visible in recent years? The idea of oneness may be a bigger illusion than I imagined. I dare to hope anyway because while I am alive, that is the direction of my striving. Peace on Purpose is us doing our part; doing better as we know better.

The Choice to Do Better

The choice to do better can be a pivotal and quite a viscerally decisive moment in one's life. We may know better for months and spend time admonishing ourselves with "shoulds". Let's stop "shoulding" on ourselves! At least be aware we are doing so.

Better to glean the wisdom gained from the "shoulding" and hold it until we are ready to use it. When we make the choice to do better based on the wisdom of knowing better, it is as if we are stepping on a newfound path of our choosing supported by self-loving courage that will better us, loved ones and All. We can extract wisdom from the nonsense happenings of life and realize a new course as we know better.

For example, I was a very heavy smoker from the age of thirteen to thirty-three. I suppressed my feelings, my voice and hurt my body. I knew better for years! I "quit" a few times with low frequency intention and observed myself in withdrawal while getting better acquainted with my habit.

After about a week, I would return to smoking with vengeance. In the process, I learned about myself and the habit I was living. For example, I could work at a job I did not really like, because I liked smoking while at work. I could spend time with people who really were not my people, because at least I was smoking. Slowly, I uncovered the veil or rather the truth beyond the haze of smoke. I used smoking to support inaction and stagnation.

And when the visceral decision to do better anchored into my body? I did not look back. Instead, the power gained from having healed younger parts of me and re-scripting hurtful belief systems into positive truths, propelled me onward with a clearer horizon. For me, that final conviction, or step in the healing process is usually in my body. For you it may be linked to emotional and/or mental sensations or thoughts that need to be reconciled last. Everyone is different and has their sacred timing.

Long before the final quitting of smoking, I did, however, stop smoking during pregnancies. Somehow, I could more easily honor the lives of my children growing inside of me than I honored my own life force back then. Sacred timing.

We are All Growing at Varying Rates

When reflecting on judgements against others I implore you to consider that though we may be similar in chronological age, there may be a great disparity between us in terms of consciousness, intellect, and simply overall intention. As rational beings we would not get angry at a kindergartener who did not understand, for example, our statements about "the ends do not justify the means."

How do we justify being angry at anyone for not understanding or for being different from us? When it comes to levels of consciousness, maybe we are in preschool and our spiritual teacher is in graduate school! Can we begin to remove the separation of the human idea of being "better than"? Are we better than a kindergartner? Really?

And if our friend's understanding of the world of finance far exceeds ours, though similar in age, our understanding may be more like high school to their graduate school knowledge. This does not equate to "better than." They simply know more about that topic than we do. We are happy to defer to them if we choose not to advance our knowledge in that area.

When we are in "upset" and judging others or self as "less than" or "more than", we may better connect if we begin to imagine us in our appropriate grade levels. This view assists us in maintaining an open heart. Now of course, if we are hiring someone for a job, we want them to be at an appropriate grade level regarding specific topics AND if we interview people who are not at certain levels, we don't have to look down on them in the process.

<u>The Crazy Mix of Life! The Soul's Curriculum</u>

Life delivers some incredible, beautiful, crazy, sad and unwelcome circumstances. Don't you wish we had a magic crystal ball to explain the workings of life on Earth? We do not have all the answers. I have developed the answers for me.

What has kept me sane is to believe that each soul has a curriculum – meaning that each being is born with a set of things that they want to experience and learn from so that there is a proclivity to live life in a way that presents a pattern of learning opportunities. The thing is, once I am born and living, I may avoid the learning opportunities. There is "choice" here in life. Free will. How we choose to be just might wield a lot of power in this life.

Please understand that as a human, I am not suggesting that any other human "deserves" the pain that comes their way as per that curriculum or choices. I am telling you that I believe this, so I don't go crazy wondering how horrible or spectacular things happen to some people and not to others etc.

In the same way as I have learned to make sense of healing and taking responsibility, by trying on this new language, so to speak, and not arguing why I do or do not accept the masculine and feminine principles applied to words, I allow myself to accept that "stuff" happens. "Curriculum happens." "Life happens."

Am I suggesting that if I were abused that I should just heal and release that reality? Yes and no. The internal machinations of me beg for light and forgiveness so I can free myself from emotional pain and mental anguish and there is a part of me that also requires justice and physical world accountability.

Therefore, I strive to reconcile the learning on all levels. The perpetrator may be in jail because I took physical world action to secure a sentencing AND I can still choose to extract wisdom from the pain of my story meaning how I came to judge myself and others. I can choose to access the healing and forgiveness required to free myself from the baggage of pain and blame. I can own the connection from the other side of the Bridge of Curiosity.

As a human, some scenarios are hard to take, especially when minors and innocents are involved. They need time to become adults as they struggle to regulate emotions thrown, sometimes violently, off balance during innocence. There is a phase in sacred timing where it is more than appropriate to rage one's pain at the Universe before opening to responsibility from an adult perspective. Sometimes the child or the inner child needs to vent. It's a human thing. Just ensure the venting is safe and appropriate.

Some people do not live long enough to heal as adults. I do not have answers for you. I have some answers for myself with which I can live.

I know that as a human being my ability to understand Divine Law will always be at a standard that challenges me by way of how I choose to be in each moment of this lifetime. I choose to keep going with heart. There is always more to learn and more to love.

Healing Like Peeling Layers of an Onion

I sometimes describe healing over time as peeling layers of an onion. Remember the first time you cut a yellow or white onion? How many tears did you shed? Though some of us are more sensitive than others to the vapors emitted by a cut onion, we hopefully do learn over time, to adapt better to this part of meal preparation!

Peeling/slicing an onion can be a metaphor for time. For example, considering how we might transform pain or ruminate when revisiting past pain. The older the onion, the more tears shed due to buildup of sulfuric compounds or rather the buildup of "resentment/pain". The fresher the onion, the less buildup, equates to fewer tears.

To avoid tears, is it enough to simply avoid old onions? If only life were that simple! The onion's age is what it is. Sometimes I begin to notice patterns in what I am learning. "This again?" How long have I been hanging out with that onion?

Another approach we can use when we realize that the onion "of our pain" is old and chock full of sulfuric acid (pain), is to ensure we use a very sharp knife when cutting. The clearer the intention and the sharper the knife used, the "cleaner the cut" the less sulfuric compounds emitted, and tears shed. That is to say, the sooner and more often we circle back, and *Reclaim, Reconcile, Reframe, and Realign* issues from our past, the better!

If you find yourself circling around an old onion, do not despair, a sharp intention goes a long way. Sometimes, a good cleansing cry goes a long way too. I trust the process.

Story Telling

How often do I find myself telling my story? Someone may ask me a simple question pertaining to the present moment and I find myself igniting a hamster wheel of motion into stories from the past that generally involve blaming others or a level of over explaining that either provides a detour for an accountability that might otherwise land in my lap or shed light on my unwillingness to let go of the pain.

In my experience, telling one's story can be part of the healing journey, and may initially be a necessary part of the healing process for some personalities. The thing is, at some point, we do become aware of the repetition and the somewhat unsettled, or uncentered sense we have of ourselves when the story is finished being shared. It is very important to be aware of the stages of telling the story and the sacred timing therein.

Initially, we share the story to reveal that we have been hurt or wronged. We have a need to reveal the pain we experienced or caused. It can be very important to give voice to the experience so to begin a dialogue with our upset. Those of us exercising the intention to heal and seeking assistance to do just that, will eventually notice in ourselves that something feels "off" when in story telling mode.

We may even become tired of hearing ourselves "prove" how we were "right," or justify our pain for example. The gift of this phase of storytelling is that it provides a spotlight on a great place to start the Peace on Purpose journey. Check in with self and trace the story patterns back to a life stage. This is our wisdom showing us where to begin if we so choose.

There is a critical moment in the healing process when our awareness keys in and begins to shift the purpose of sharing the story. In becoming accountable to forgiveness and gratitude the energy of our story shifts from being about us as victims to being a story told only with the intention to assist others.

Instead of telling a story with a "look at my pain" which may be a necessary part of the process for a time, we instead begin to offer the wisdom of the story for others to embrace, should they so choose. When we find ourselves sharing the wisdom of our stories as an offering to others, regardless of how the gift is received, our hamster wheels cease to spin. As an audience to our own words, we listen to ourselves through the stillness of peace.

<u>Mourning to Morning Milestones</u>

As we journey along the Time Circle, we become aware of memories that are painful, poignant and challenging to release. As we age, we receive various messaging regarding time: "time is an illusion", "time heals all wounds," and "it's just a matter of time." If we are holding on to regrets as we age, our burdens may become heavier than our weighted hearts can carry. We acknowledge the milestones in our lives that we have been mourning. As we allow ourselves the *mourning* milestones process, we can embrace *morning* milestones to begin anew with the levity of wisdom and forgiveness flowing through our hearts. Often easier said than done AND well worth the endeavor.

Let's briefly visit Jim's story: Jim disliked his daughter's choice of a husband. He felt Janaya was too good for her husband and was also displeased that the couple did not share the same faith. Jim went through the motions, attending holidays and sharing the occasional meal with his son-in-law but over time began to express his displeasure openly.

Little by little, Janaya made different holiday plans and had excuses as to why they could not meet Jim for dinner. As the grandchildren were born, Jim found himself to be somewhat of an outsider in his own family. Janaya's mother spent a lot of time with her grandchildren while Jim stubbornly chose to remain at home.

Eventually Jim got past his prejudices and was lucky to have his family available to him; they never closed him off. He did that to himself. After nearly eight years in self-imposed exile, Jim missed out on appreciating his grandchildren as babies and building relationships with them as preschoolers. Making up for "lost time", Jim's family cohesively fostered him into his role as grandfather and father-in-law and life carried on with togetherness. As Jim aged, he experienced what we call "mourning milestones" because he realized what he had missed and regretted his past decisions.

What can we say about mourning milestones? Whether or not the events were in our control, things occurred, decisions were made, and life moved on. We have the choice to grip the mourning or to release it to the dawn of a new day.

The nature of deep retrospective regret is a heavy burden. If we allow ourselves to mourn the loss of these milestones and forgive ourselves, we free the wisdom of what we have learned from the painful baggage we have been carting around and allow that wisdom to pervade our hearts.

Wise hearts share exuberantly, like the Grinch whose heart grew three sizes! With understanding, healing and forgiveness we transform mourning the milestones into Morning Milestones. A new day to be present to each moment with gratitude for what is. Whether or not one is able to reconnect with family, as in the example of Jim, we cannot save each other from the pain of learning or the "game" of the illusion of time.

How many of us have lost years with loved ones and do not see a reconciliation possible? It is so very painful! And, if we spend our energy on mourning for too long, meaning, when we finally have the capacity to strive for Morning Milestones and resist the healing, then our life force suffers and all the people who could have received blessings from us, will go without. We do not envy the position of mourning milestones. The depth of loss is almost limitless. We can, however, support our hearts to grow so to give and receive more love no matter the outcome.

In my experience, Morning Milestones are exercised by elders (at any age) who diffuse their hearts with wisdom gleaned and give back to younger generations in ways that the latter appreciates and not in ways that the elder deems more important. To open to Morning Milestones, we are open to continued personal growth knowing that we do better as we know better.

Chapter 2

Life Stages of Development Around the Time Circle & User Instructions

Now that we are equipped with the considerations for the journey, let's get an overview of the life stages around the Time Circle with the intention of assisting our self-awareness. The Peace on Purpose journey involves one or hopefully many treks around the Wisdom Time Circle.

The trek can be a future and/or retrospective visit to the chronological human development stages of one's life as represented by each cardinal point.

The life stages of birth, adolescence, adulthood and elderhood are described in detail by influential 20th Century psychoanalyst Erik Erikson in his book, *8 Stages of Development*. After maturing in the womb, humans are born and continue to develop as they grow. Erikson presented an explanation for the turning points individuals face through life phases that affect their psychosocial experiences as they develop physically.

How one moves through and reconciles the phases within themselves determines the correlating self-impressions one has, both conscious and subconscious.

It is not important to memorize each phase for the Peace on Purpose journey. I refer to Erikson to support us in highlighting aspects of life stages to perhaps spark a memory or deeper understanding of where we have been, are now and where we are going.

As we walk the life path our inner responses to experiences begin to script the messages we will tell ourselves even when no one, including us, is actively listening. The script is determined by the filters we create in response and/or reaction to what others reflect to us.

For example, we have the experience that our babysitter Sue is not paying attention to us while we explain how our day was. We are seven years old, and we may perceive Sue not listening to us by the "lack of interest" as defined by her body language, eye contact, or focus on something else, for example, to mean that we are inferior and unimportant. That is one basic conclusion that is common for this scenario.

Aware of it or not, as we live our lives, day to day, we are authoring the script from which we are living. By walking the Time Circle, with intention, we can script from a conscious place and polish any areas in the past that may be lacking clarity, desire acknowledgement or have been awaiting forgiveness for years and years. Hence, the reason why we may need to return to younger stages is to invite ourselves to update self-impressions and edit the script accordingly.

We will go back when we know better, so we can do better! *Reclaim*, *Reconcile* (forgive ourselves and others), *Reframe* the old messaging, for example, and *Realign* to the truth as we move forward.

Erikson did not attribute cardinal points to his presentation of life stages. When I wrote the paper for grad school back in 1999 entitled "The Way of the Sacred Directions", I included the life stages to promote the understanding of one's development along a chronological path with the hope that the stages would inspire a recall to broken parts of me that yearned for realignment and/or to parts of me expressing gratitude.

I am sharing this information with you merely to inspire recall with compassion and in some cases, an enhanced understanding of what a life stage is working to balance. This is for your consideration. Life goes on with the striving for continued growth and balance. Entelechy is relentless! Entelechy: *The realization of potential.*

The East:

The east has four stages:

<u>Trust vs. Mistrust</u> covers birth to about one and a half years old and adjusts within the caregiver relationship, generally the primary caregiver connection. The goal of this phase is <u>HOPE</u>.

<u>Autonomy vs Shame/Doubt</u> covers the toddler months and adjusts within relationship with the parents and what they are reflecting. Goal: <u>WILL POWER</u>.

<u>Initiative vs Guilt</u> covers ages three to six years old. This stage adjusts within the basic family construct. Goal: <u>PURPOSE</u>.

<u>Industry vs. Inferiority</u> covers ages six to eleven and adjusts within one's neighborhood and school environment. Goal: <u>COMPETENCE</u>.

<u>The South:</u>

<u>Identity vs Identity Confusion</u> covers adolescence and adjusts amongst peer groups and models of leadership. Goal: <u>FIDELITY</u>.

<u>The West:</u>

<u>Intimacy vs isolation</u> are the years of young adulthood and adjust amongst partners in friendships, sex, competition and cooperation. Goal: <u>LOVE</u>.

<u>Generativity vs Self-Absorption</u> are the adult years which adjust amongst divided labor and shared households. Goal: <u>CARE</u>.

<u>The North:</u>

<u>Integrity vs Despair</u>. This stage comprises the elder years and reconciles around "My kind" versus "Humankind". The goal is <u>WISDOM</u>. In short, is life centered around me or am I generative and being of service to others?

<u>Wisdom Time Circle Set Up and User Instructions</u>

I am open and willing to grow in new directions. This was part of the vow I wrote for my marriage which I now apply to being married to myself.

I am open to growing in new directions and as such I am willing to explore me as I have been doing.

What else is there to consider when embarking on this journey? We must also be willing to "deal" with our puzzle of us. We may find some incongruence that might trick us like the image of Picasso style heads on Monet bodies when completing life puzzles. We may think we have a completed puzzle because all the pieces fit together until and if we look more closely. Are we ready?

The next sections involve "user manual" information from set up, to taking our first steps around the circle, followed by intentions and actions, ending with guidelines for witnessing the process. If you are the type of person who would rather read about the "how to" at the end of a book, I suggest you skim forward to Mike's Peace on Purpose Story in Chapter Three and return to this chapter another time.

Setting Up the Time Circle

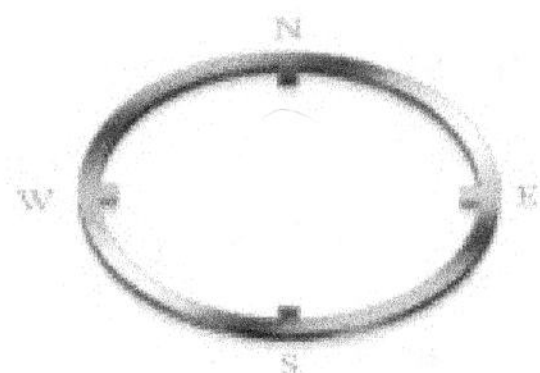

To start, have four delineating objects of similar size (five if you want something in the center) like rocks or gemstones for example. Use a phone app compass to determine the location of the cardinal points. Place a rock, or an item important to you that is easy to manipulate at each point creating at least a four or five-foot minimum diameter for the circle.

Note that the diameter of the Time Circle should be guided by the space you are using and whether you are circling in a temporary or permanent space. Ideally, I prefer a minimum of ten feet diameter because I like to walk slowly around the circle and not feel dizzy. More on this later. As we are working with intention, the circle can be palm sized to thirty feet in diameter. We all have a varying presentation.

After the set-up is complete, walk around the circle, clockwise, a few times to see what part we are drawn to. I like to do this to establish that I feel connected to the Time Circle before I begin the journey. Note that once we have developed a well-worn inner path for this work, the external circle may not be necessary.

Over time, the Peace on Purpose Circle is within us. The more we walk the journey, the more we will realize that the Time Circle is within.

Personally, sometimes a quick set up and walk, feeling my feet on the ground, is what I need to get out of my "hamster wheeling" thoughts.

We can create a permanent area for the circle or set up camp as needed whether indoors or outdoors. Be creative! As long as the path is delineated by the cardinal points and the center is acknowledged as a blank space or has an item in the center spot, it is ready to go.

When I have outdoor space, or designated indoor space, I like having a permanent circle so I can use it weekly or daily as walking meditation whereby I maintain awareness of how I am doing in general.

<u>Simple Start</u>

After a quick set up, what may work for many of us is to simply walk the Time Circle clockwise for several laps and intuitively stop. Note where we end up standing and consider the life stages represented by that area. We allow thoughts and memories to bubble up. Some make us wonder and smile, others may pool a few tears or feel nothing. This may be the process for us for a long time.

We may also be inspired to look at photos of ourselves during the course of our life. The images are a Time Circle journey. For many of us, reading through the stories in this book and reviewing ourselves and pictures around the Time Circle may be as far as we go with this book.

We make an authentic start that may look different for each of us and trust the process. We have no judgement or expectations on each other's outcomes. We support each other in walking the positive healing path that resonates in our sacred timing.

<u>Sue's "Getting Started" Story</u>

Sue set up a Time Circle in her yard and walked around it a few times. She found herself feeling silly and disconnected. She decides to go through her computer for downloaded photos in addition to the boxes of pictures that she had been saving to arrange in albums.

Sue reviews the life stages and chooses one or two photos of herself from each stage. She places the photos on the ground, in their corresponding life stage locations around the circle.

As she walks the Time Circle again, equipped with photo inspired memories, she touches moments of gratitude and reaches out to younger parts of herself, connecting with acknowledgement. Sue finds herself walking the circle in gratitude and speaks in the NOW to younger selves.

To her ten-year-old self, "I feel your sadness when grandpa died." "He was one of your biggest fans!" "I am also a big fan of you" Sue hears herself admit. "You learned how to play chess with grandpa and to appreciate poetry." "I love this part of us that we have taught to my kids because you were so lovingly open to learn from him instead of running off to a friend's house." "Thank you for having such heart and for taking that time." "Your love has kept grandpa in our lives by continuing the poetry and chess legacies."

Sue might uncover other messages along the way that feel important to be spoken and acknowledged. She might uncover an upset that had long since been forgotten and decide to touch that poignancy as well.

To Sue's surprise, her ten-year-old self reveals anger that she had not been permitted to visit grandpa in the hospital before he died. Adult Sue had forgotten about that pain. "Ten-year-old Sue, how can I help?" Sue asks. The younger Sue decides that she wants to send a card to grandpa explaining how she wished she could have hugged him one more time.

Adult Sue with little Sue in her heart, takes quiet time to sit with paper, crayons and magic markers and creates the special card for grandpa. The poignant energy running through Sue's body released the pain of the inner ten-year-old and warms her heart peacefully. Together they created a beautiful poem of love and appreciation.

Permanent Time Circle

The photo above is representative of a small permanent circle of about three feet diameter. This is for someone who wants one as a ritual place to stand and ponder. Walking a small circle makes one a bit dizzy and is not recommended. Use the photo as a guide and make the circle much bigger! At least six feet.

If a permanent circle is chosen, we can fill in all the circular path spaces between cardinal points with smaller items so that the whole diameter is delineated. This is the benefit of not needing to dismantle the circle. If we don't want to fill in the spaces, we can simply choose four or five large rocks or crystals; the fifth one for the center if you choose not to leave it empty.

Ideally allow for a minimum of six feet in diameter, if possible, so we can easily have the experience of walking and standing around it. I love to work with a ten-foot plus diameter when possible.

Temporary Time Circle

I have been known to create a Time Circle on the sand at the beach with five shells or rocks using only a three-foot diameter to illustrate to a small group. In this case the movement happens more by dragging one's finger around in the sand. I have also been on a walking trail with a client and simply found some stones, pieces of tree branches and created a quick Time Circle on the spot as well.

Either way we go, until we have walked the Time Circle more than several times and feel connected to the process, initially, having a bigger space so our whole body can do the mindful walk around the circle is ideal as we take in the new experience and trust our instincts. It is the quality of our intention and commitment to the process that will serve overall.

Mini Time Circle

It is possible to use a mini version of the Time Circle. Ideally, after being well acquainted with the process, it will be easier to use the small version. Unless one cannot physically handle the larger Time Circle set up and walk, the alternative is available. The mini Time Circle can be set in a sand garden if one wants the sensory experience of sand or use a digital or paper image with the cardinal points demarcated. We can run a finger around the mini Time Circle and proceed with the process according to the guidelines.

Placement of the Cardinal Points

Before we place the items that will represent the cardinal points (and center piece if we so choose) have a compass handy or open an app on a smartphone. Decide the radius and design as it flows for each of us. For example, using two-inch seashells as cardinal point markers on a twenty-foot diameter Time Circle may or may not flow. As we place the items that represent the cardinal points, we place them with care and intention, reminding ourselves what each point represents to facilitate and inspire the process.

The Basic Recap:

East is for Birth – new beginnings (birth to just before adolescence)

South is Adolescence – discovery (adolescence just up to adulthood)

West is Adulthood – responsibility, identification of and harvest of the blessings of who I am (adulthood)

North is Elderhood – wisdom – how one is giving back to others (Elder years)

Center – May represent Wholeness (Receiving the blessings of the session and/or connection to ALL)

North to east – Gratitude reality – awareness of the blessings that were present all along.

The center of the circle for me represents wholeness and oneness with the All of life. How does that resonate for you? Occasionally, when I feel like I am shifting my sense of self into alignment, I like to take time to stand or sit in the center of the circle. When I am there, I imagine I am being charged up like my cell phone battery. Recharged and standing with newly found alignment with the blessings received in the session.

Maintain the area to be esthetically pleasing, for example, free of weeds, if outside, or unrelated debris when possible. Treat the healing path as sacred space.

<u>Considerations for Walking the Peace on Purpose Time Circle</u>

INTENTION

Before walking the circle, we sit, stand and/or journal quietly. We may choose to review photos of our life stages. We state our session intentions out loud. Ideally the intention is to choose to heal and/or express gratitude "for the highest good of all concerned." We listen closely to our voice as we state the intention. Note that if we are working with a witness, they will hear us as well.

Consequently, our witness will also state their intention (more on this in the "Witness" section below.) The "highest good" phrase is to say that we are taking steps towards healing and since we may not know best using our "mind," we are also turning over the highest good of the experience to be co-created by Source. This helps us tackle the "I am right" voice so we remain open to the possibilities.

What is Source when I use the term "co-create with Source"? Source would be whatever god we pray to, or some higher power. If we are an atheist, then maybe think of it as simply being open to the highest healing or way of being as a human. Perhaps it is our "higher selves" which is an example of human intellect and physiology striving for its best self; for instance, the part that is available to more than five senses, even if we cannot imagine it yet. This intention allows us to open to possibilities.

Example: "It is my intention to step into gratitude and to reconcile with any aspect of me that is revealed to me as I circle my story. I do this to the best of my ability and for the highest good of all concerned." Stated more simply "I am in" with the understanding of the deeper meaning which is to be open to knowing that our "mind" may not know the best healing strategy.

CHOICE

By making the intention to walk the Peace on Purpose Time Circle we then choose to put the Intention into Action. It is imperative that our willingness to combine intention and choice/action is honest. Let's face it, if we are not serious about the journey, then why bother?

What we get from the experience is a direct reflection of the quality and consciousness of our intention. If we are looking to prove to ourselves that healing is a foolish investment that never works anyway, we can easily prove that right? I would venture to guess that we may already have "mastered" or "mistressed" that belief system if that is the case.

What is really at risk should we choose to move forward with authentic healing intention? It is our choice to set Intention and to take action to support the intention. Consider that the outcome or rather continued learning may look different than what we pictured. The Universe meets us when we set an intention and take action to support that intention. How does the Universe respond? Sometimes it makes for a very interesting story.

ACTION

We have set heart-felt intention, we make the choice to journey and then put our intention into action. If we believe in prayer, in my opinion, this is prayer in action. If we do not believe in prayer, then perhaps we can consider this as an opening to being a more conscious human with a focus on what we are manifesting in the moment. Might that work for us? Let's go a bit deeper. Choosing to take action is great! **How we behave as we act is also of great importance.**

THE HOW

How we show up is just as important to note as us simply showing up. An exercise I used to run with clients is that I would ask one to hand me a water bottle, for example. Typically, they would hand over the water bottle distractedly and I would take it with a "thanks" spoken off to the side. Next, I would ask them to gently "toss" a water bottle to me.

I would then recap: "The task was to hand me a water bottle and then toss one to me." "In both cases, the task was completed, right?" Then it was my turn, and I would have the client ask me for a water bottle. The first time I would hand it to them with me looking a bit distracted. The second time I would toss it to them instead of handing it over. I asked them to acknowledge that both times, they got what they asked for. Then, I would have them ask me one more time. The third time I would walk towards them, holding the water bottle with both my hands, in a way to convey that the water bottle was very important. Then, I would hand it to them, slowly, while attempting to make eye contact and I would speak "Here is a water bottle for you." At this point, the client would have the experience of three very different methods of me getting a water bottle to them in addition to having their own experience of two ways of getting the water to me.

Before starting a full discussion, the client is then asked to give me a water bottle for the last time, so they can hand one to me "formally". Following that exchange, the client is asked to share how it feels to both give and receive in the three different ways. This is generally a simple discussion that anchors important experience in their bodies with seeds of choice and memory.

The nuance of the HOW can be a fun interaction. The final conversation with the client was for them to describe HOW it felt to give and receive in three ways. The HOW we act with intention is critically important, especially when we are also giving to ourselves.

Is it okay if we are in a place where we may "throw or toss" our intention into the Time Circle? Absolutely! We are then still exactly where we need to be on the Peace on Purpose journey. It is okay and important to be aware that we are doing so. Awareness is key. I invite us to be aware of "how" we are taking action. Are we approaching the journey trying not to be present? Flinging our intention to "get it over with"? Walking the circle with reverence and presence? Take note of the approach.

Awareness may offer insight as to what is going on inside of us and how we are feeling. Some people feel uncomfortable the first few times they walk the Time Circle while others mesh with the steps with ease. Either way, and everything in between is okay because we have the intention to do our highest good/best! How we show up is just as important as showing up and the clues gleaned as to how we are feeling are priceless.

Time Circle Witness

There is a voice that doesn't use words. Listen. ~ Rumi

We are encouraged to have a witness who is neutral. This is a person who is comfortable with silence and focusing their awareness on another person. This person resists telling us their story and does not try to "fix" us or our story. We, along with the witness, are actively learning the difference between the voice of wisdom versus the voice that expresses fears. We listen for wisdom and note the "tell" in our bodies when wisdom is experienced. We might feel a warmth in our gut or find ourselves listening deeply and tilting our head to the left. We are taking note of the tell; how our bodies signal to us that wisdom is beckoning.

We may also choose to walk the Time Circle without a witness. I think it can be a light-hearted way to touch or locate the first layers of healing to walk without witness. Often what we uncover during a session may be great for discussing with a therapist or coach soon thereafter for a deeper dive into feelings.

Until we are solid in awareness and practice of our inner affirming witness, walking the Time Circle solo may be challenging. It can also be exciting to ignite a sense of "play" from the energy of childhood. We are encouraged to take the process slowly and be cautious because relationship with self is precious.

If we find ourselves swimming in emotion without moving easily into gratitude, we may need professional assistance to further and more deeply address what is unfolding. If a licensed therapist is not required, solid friends, with hearts of service, are golden support. See the section on "Witnessing the Peace on Purpose Time Circle Journey" for witness guidelines.

Guidelines for Using the Time Circle:

Please read through the guidelines below for a deeper understanding of using the Time Circle. AND if we are not ready to take the deeper first step, it is perfectly acceptable to approach a walk around the Time Circle with the spirit of: *Hi! It's me, Giulia Cappelli. It is very nice and a bit overwhelming to revisit and recall you, parts of me on this new journey. My intention is to simply walk around the makeshift Time Circle and invite connection with you in this new way. I may do this several times before I decide to review directions further. In fact, I may choose to stand at each section in silence and just be with myself and parts of me that may rise to my mind and memories.* We each follow our sacred timing.

- By now we have set up our Time Circle and maybe have walked around it a few times to connect with how it feels and

to note what area we feel drawn to.
- Before starting the journey, we do a quick review of the meanings of the cardinal points and the definitions of Reclaim, Reframe, Reconcile and Realign.
- We look over the considerations for the journey to assist us to be in the mindset of taking responsibility:
    - I am Right
    - Crossing the Bridge of Curiosity
    - Assessment versus Judgement
    - Own the Connection
    - The Choice to Do Better
    - We Are All Growing at Various Rates
    - The Crazy Mix of Life! Soul's Curriculum
    - Healing like Peeling Layers of an Onion
    - Story Telling
    - Mourning/Morning Milestones
- We, along with our witness, if we have one, will state our Intentions for the session out loud.
- Note that we are making a choice to support our Intention by taking Action to walk the Time Circle.
- Be conscious of the HOW we approach the session – note our demeanor.
- Be gentle with ourselves and be open to possibilities.
- Walk around the circle clockwise a few times and note the location of where we are drawn, in this case, where are we standing when we intuitively stop walking and stand still.
    - The practice of walking the circle is to engage the body and the mind into thinking and feeling that we are communing with self at various ages. That we are listening to what is going on inside of us.
- Using a physical set up tends to facilitate the experience happening in the Now. We want healing to happen in the

Now which is why we speak TO and FROM aspects of us at various life stages as opposed to speaking "about" them.

○ Ask ourselves why our body stopped at a particular area of the circle. What does that area represent in life stages and general meaning I.e., new beginnings, discovery, responsibility, elder wisdom? What message might we have for ourselves regarding that stage? From there we intuit a starting point for the session. We might, however, join the session already knowing about which we are upset and who we are blaming. What story do we hear ourselves telling?

The basic cardinal point meanings:

- East is for Birth – *new beginning*
- South is Adolescence – *discover*
- West is Adulthood – *responsibility*
- North is Elderhood – *wisdom*
- North to east is Gratitude – *transformation from Mourning to Morning Milestones*

Let us review the meaning of the four R's:

- *Reclaim* is to pick up any lost pieces of self that may have been left in the past.
- *Reframe* is to infuse belief systems with truth.
- *Reconcile* is to bathe the experience in forgiveness.
- *Realign* is to mesh gratitude with the truth and clarity that forgiveness provides.

We have crossed over the Bridge of Curiosity and find ourselves approaching the Time Circle. We state our intention and walk around the perimeter of the circle and become still. We notice which cardinal point we are near when we stop walking and consider the meaning while also considering what our body/mind/heart is telling us. We use the questions below to assist the process. We are open to possibilities!

Guiding Questions/Steps for Time Circle Session

Both participant and witness, if there is one, speak their Intention aloud. For example, "My intention for this session is to connect more with myself, or my inner child, *for the highest good.*" Witness, for example: "My intention for this session is to support the wisdom being shared by the participant in a way that serves their highest good."

First question: *What's going on with me? Why am I here? What happened? When I close my eyes or quiet my thoughts, what comes to mind? What pattern of story do I find myself spewing especially when I am talking to myself? What part of my pattern is the spotlight showing?*

Second question: *Who or what is to blame? What aspect of self (past or future age of me) am I addressing?* "Reclaim". Or simply *What is present?*

Third question: *After I spew judgements about how others are wrong or how I may be wrong, what's at risk if I realize I can see the situation in a different way? In other words, if I am operating from a place of care, what could I have done or thought differently? If I were to give up my position of being Right, what am I afraid may be true about myself? And then, what is the truth?* "Reframe."

Fourth question: *What am I forgiving?* Practice the forgiveness statements until the words that cause us to catch our breath with heart and emotion are found. Then state the truth, for example reframing the old beliefs and embrace the truth. "Reconcile."

Fifth question: Have you made any inner or outer agreements with self? What is the plan according to the agreement? Have a follow-up plan in place so as to honor agreements.

Sixth question: *What is the gratitude reality?* "Realign." Address the status of Mourning Milestones transforming to Morning Milestones.

Seventh question: *How complete are we with the session?* Let's think about it. We can jot down ideas for another session if we become aware of more.

End of Session

Gratitude. At the end of a session, we breathe in the gratitude reality a second time and acknowledge ourselves for our self-loving efforts. Remember, "growth is a process". If we have a witness, we acknowledge them for their service!

Session Assessment & Considerations

Assess how we feel at the end of the session. Are there things we wish we had done differently? Do we want to incorporate self-forgiveness for these potential judgements or perhaps simply jot the ideas down in a journal for the next time? Let's be gentle with ourselves. Before we know it, the process will come naturally, and we won't even need to look at any questions. We will flow with intention.

Is our witness open to feedback from us about how they can improve their demeanor as a witness? If so, let's be careful to speak in "I" statements so we are not shaming them.

For example, "During the session, when I saw you staring off into the distance when I was talking to my inner eight-year-old, I felt like I was boring you; like you were not really with me." "Is what I am sharing true?"

This type of comment keeps the focus on what the participant experienced indirectly as opposed to accusing the witness of purposefully wanting the participant to feel like their share was boring or that the witness was daydreaming.

Use feedback that does not use accusatory language.

Don't say: "You ignored me!" Instead, say: "I felt ignored" which is preferred and good feedback. In this example the participant learns that they may have a fear operating regarding boring people in their lives or just of being a boring person, for example, and the witness learns to explore alternatives of where to focus their eyes when a participant is speaking to convey attentiveness.

Are we open to receiving feedback from the witness? For example, the witness may share that they "wondered" if we left out some information that they felt we had wanted to share with our inner child because they thought they saw us hesitate, for example. This is good feedback as long as we are not being accused of not sharing on purpose etc.

Perhaps we might resonate with their "wondering" and admit that we were in fact feeling shy, for example. This clarifying exchange can assist our process as a participant because our witness can ask us if there was anything they could have done differently that would have worked better for us.

When it comes to feedback- tread with care. Let's give each other the space to learn responsible ways of speaking to one another that assists us both.

We may enter the Time Circle several times regarding one matter until we find the "way in" to our heart to support the Reclaim, Reframe, Reconcile and Realign. Sacred timing! We deserve it! Did we feel complete at the end of the session, or was there more? It is important to note so we can go back in or agree to return within a specific time frame.

Healing starts with us. What fuels our journey is the quality of our intentions, and the overall willingness we have to navigate through and liberate ourselves from the judgements, blame and limiting belief systems that we may have worked so hard to cultivate.

Let's thank the Time Circle space. If we are using a temporary circle, we return the area to its regular state with gratitude. If we have a permanent site, we discover our own way to thank the space for its part in the process.

Thank self and our witness, if we have one.

Journey Guidelines for Witnessing

We know that the quality of our Witness is a critical element of this journey if we choose to have one. A witness strives to be a neutral and supportive observer who may or may not speak during the process. HOW the witness shows up to witness is just as important as their witnessing! Consider that even we, as a participant, are a witness: when sharing the Peace on Purpose circle experience as a participant, we are also a witness to ourselves.

It is imperative that both the participant and the witness use the viewpoint of a "play therapist" who would observe a child play so that the child, or in this case the participant, does not feel judged and is not inclined to try to please the observer.

This may seem extreme and let's think about it. Especially when we were young, if someone praised us for how well we recited a poem, for example, might we be motivated to do so again for more praise? Now this may not be true for us individually, and can we imagine how it may have motivated some? Ideally, a person can draw their own conclusions about how they are doing without having to be compared to others or getting their value rated by others.

A non-qualitative way to comment for example is if we see someone drawing a scene of a house, grass, trees and mountains, we will simply state what we see them doing I.e. "I see you using the brown crayon as you trace the tree trunks". "You have drawn three trees next to the house". "I see you added mountains, yes?" (Check in for clarification in case those were not mountains).

Consider this, as soon as the witness makes qualifying statements like "I love these trees!" versus "Tell me about the trees you have drawn", the participant might want to please their witness versus do what feels right for themself. And yes, if that happens, that would be considered part of the participant's journey in life AND that is not what Peace on Purpose circle is here to evoke. If it happens, please be aware. How often is someone being authentic versus wanting to please to establish a measure of their self-worth?

Silence with appropriate eye contact is often the best support. If a witness speaks, they should ask open ended questions of the person they are supporting, remembering that the participant has their own answers/wisdom, inside of them.

If the witness is a close friend of the participant, it can be tricky to maintain neutrality. As a close friend who knows a lot of information about the participant, the witness must be extra careful not to convey judgement to the participant in the way they word questions and be hyper considerate of the way the participant might receive the message coming from them.

Remember, this is a process. It is rare that someone has ill intentions and good friendships are precious. Tread carefully!

The witness is committed to revering the participant's relationship with themself and to clarifying understanding. They interject if they see an opportunity for clarification OR that the participant may be damaging their relationship with self. The witness sees the participant's relationship with self as sacred and looks for gratitude moments to invite the participant to claim.

The witness understands the "Considerations for the Journey":

- I am Right
- Bridge of Curiosity
- Assessment versus Judgement
- Own the Connection
- The Choice to Do Better
- We Are All Growing at Varying Rates
- The Crazy Mix of Life! Soul's Curriculum
- Healing Like Peeling Layers of an Onion
- Story Telling
- Mourning/Morning Milestones

Examples of questions a witness may ask:

What is coming up for you?

What part of you are you thinking of? How old are they? How would you describe them right now?

What do you want to say to that part of you?

What does that part of you want to say to you? Is there anything they want from you?

How can I best support you as you talk to that part? Shall I stand behind you? At your side?

The witness simply states what is: *I see you reaching out to your three-year-old self." "How complete are you with this exchange?*

What stage of telling the story are you in right now? Blame, accountability and/or sharing wisdom? It is certainly okay if one needs to tell their story for a time from the standpoint of blame, just acknowledge the stage and embrace the sacred timing.

What agreement are you making to the younger/older aspect of self? Let's be specific as to what you agree to, so we account for the commitment.

The witness silently stands next to the participant and takes a few cleansing breaths as the witness waits and listens.

How present are you with this process right now? Are you willing to proceed with your choice to continue this activity?

The witness walks up to the participant, makes eye contact, mirrors their posture, takes a breath and gently repositions themself in supportive silence.

Let's be gentle with ourselves as witnesses. These guidelines are here to guide us as we are present in the NOW for the participant. Take the suggestions without getting lost in our minds. If in doubt, take a breath, open our hearts and simply listen with a body posture that supports our intention.

Time Circle Disclaimer

Ideally, this practice is intended to be executed with reverence and to be supported/witnessed by someone trained as a therapist or coach to best serve the intentions and actions of the participant. That said, you can choose a very good and trusted friend to witness. Whoever witnesses should review the Considerations for the Journey in Chapter One and the section on Witness Guidelines.

If you choose to work the Time Circle on your own, then YOU ensure that you are also aware of the Witness Guidelines so that YOU are cultivating an inner supportive presence and voice. Take your time with the process.

You are encouraged to take any issues or feelings that you uncover to a professional for further support should you feel unsettled or unfinished with the process. Should you find yourself overwhelmed with emotions and need a grounding check in, please text or call 988 a national crisis lifeline 988lifeline.org or your local emergency 911 equivalent. Support is important.

This practice is not in any way to reflect that of the sacred Native American Medicine Wheel Traditions. I am not Native American, nor have I had the honor of being initiated to a status of such sacred tradition. That stated, I am aware that the circle concept in ancient cultures in particular, the native people, the medicine wheel is explored to promote balance and also refers to cardinal points and stages of one's life cycle.

I prefer a circle to a linear timeline because the coaching strategy involves circling forward or back to various times of one's life. I explain a little in the foreword that at the University of Santa Monica (USM), when I was in graduate school in 1999, I wrote a paper entitled "The Way of the Sacred Directions." The coaching strategy describes a person's healing journey around a circle based on the cardinal points and developmental stages of a human being as the latter was part of the curriculum at USM.

I embrace the circular patterning to a linear approach for timelines because it represents Mother Earth, wholeness and the feminine essence for ancient peoples, which resonates for me. The cardinal points remind me that I am of this physical world and to check in with the deeper meaning of the corresponding life stages; what I have experienced in life in terms of emotion, belief system, forgiveness and gratitude.

I bow to the wisdom of the native peoples' way of being. I feel a depth of compassion for the hardship they have endured. How my physical world ancestors continue to assault their rights and culture because in my opinion, people have forgotten who we truly are. Instead of remembering and becoming, many of us seek to annihilate the best parts of being human as represented by the tenets of the native way of being.

There is a lot of information available regarding the practice of the medicine wheel and the differences expressed depending on the tribe. I encourage you to explore with reverence. A starting point is the Native Voices site(nlm.nih.gov/nativevoices/exhibition/healing-ways/medicine-ways/medicine-wheel.html) To share a bit more about the medicine wheel, in general, know that some tribes may ascribe other meanings to the cardinal points based on their tribal values, beliefs and stories.

The four directions: north, east, south and west also correlate potentially to the following depending on the tribe:

- Seasons: Winter, spring, summer and fall
- Life stages: Infant/birth, child/youth, adult/parent, Elder/death and grandparents
- Elements: Air, fire, water and earth
- Aspects of life: Physical, mental, spiritual and emotional
- Ceremonial plants: Sage, cedar, sweet grass and tobacco
- Celestial bodies: Sun, Earth, moon and stars
- Animals: Eagle, buffalo, wolf and bear

I recognize that there may be similarities between my approach and the medicine wheel way. Having never been taught the latter, I can only claim that I am honored to intuit a way of being that is in any way akin to native peoples. When asked where I come from, after stating the Italian heritage my physical world body conveys, I say that intuitively I feel more that I am a Native American Spirit in an Italian American body.

<u>Finding Peace on Purpose Circle of Something Else</u>

Keep in mind that if we like the set up and using a physical space to ponder inner thoughts the circle can be used to honor the beginning, middle, and end including the gratitude of "happenings" in life. We can stand at the Time Circle, for example, as we start a new job and imagine how we will circle our story as a new employee. We can use the circle to honor a new relationship. This would be a tool to keep us more present to doing our part in maintaining awareness and take responsibility for our part of the relationship or new job.

Consider the life stage phases. For example, how is the relationship progressing with respect to trust, autonomy, initiative, intimacy etc. Maybe it's better to be simple about it – we can just ask ourselves how we are doing based on "new beginnings", "discovery", "responsibility" and "wisdom".

If we like this style of presence and focus on our life, we can use this system as a catalyst to maintain timely consideration for the important parts we identify in our life that we want to be grateful for and heal and grow. It becomes a way to walk the circle and check in with us.

Using the Time Circle to address current life events and endeavors like projects, new jobs, relationships can become a very powerful practice in cultivating the awareness of HOW we want to be with respect to the varying happenings in our lives.

Chapter 3
Mike's Peace on Purpose Story

Let's share Mike's story so we have an example of how one works this process from start to finish. In this example, Mike is working with a coach. There are several other stories that will be shared in Chapter Six. Some of the stories focus on the Gratitude Reality of life while others may illuminate some process work of extracting wisdom from around the Time Circle.

Meet Mike at age thirty. Picture the circular timeline with compass points that delineate life's developmental stages: birth, adolescence, adulthood and elderhood. Everyone has pivotal instances in their life, whether they evoke pain and/or gratitude, that positively or negatively affected their self-talk and/or molded how they respond or react.

Mike stands around the circle at the thirty-year-old marker in the section of the west, Adulthood. What's Mike's issue? Recently at work, Mike's co-workers failed to invite him to a gathering following the culmination of an important project. Mike finds himself feeling triggered. He has noticed that he often gets upset when he feels "left out". He resents his co-workers.

Mike sets out, through work with a coach, to *Reclaim, Reframe, Reconcile and Realign* with a younger aspect of self because he recognizes that the feeling of being "left out" started when he was in elementary school. In terms of set up, Mike is working with a coach at a designated location, in this case, indoors at home due to the weather and logistics. Please note I do not advocate creating Time Circles in the office unless HR agrees and advocates for corporate Peace on Purpose work.

At the session start, the coach states intention to be present and to support Mike's experience. Mike also says an intention aloud. "I am open to understanding why I feel left out now and when I was younger. I don't want to feel this way unnecessarily." Then Mike walks around the Time Circle until his body stops. Mike is still near the south point which represents "Discovery".

Mike recalls feeling unliked by school friends when he was around seven years old. These were the experiences that may cause him to be negatively triggered still, when at age thirty, co-workers forget to include him in an after-work dinner invite, for example. Did they purposefully not invite him?

How might life be positively different moving forward if consolation and support were exchanged between present Mike and seven-year-old Mike? If Mike did not get what he needed back when he was a seven-year-old, he can take responsibility as an adult to accomplish it Now. It is a choice. We may wish that Mike's parents, teachers, guardians and school friends had saved him from upset as a child. We don't know if they did try or ever noticed.

Whose responsibility is it now that Mike is now having issues with his co-workers? Hmm. Of course, I think we can agree that it is always welcomed for people responsible for minors especially, to do what is needed to "make things right" and/or apologize at the time of an occurrence. Let's face it, most of the time, we are flying solo and surrounded by slews of fantastical intentions, including our own. In the end, and at the point of awareness, we, as adults, have the responsibility to nurture ourselves to wholeness.

As an aside, Kudos to all the mental health workers, clinicians, behavior technicians and teachers who hold space for healing, especially the children and teens who are struggling due to severe circumstances.

I briefly worked as a mental health worker at an outpatient facility for children and adolescents, as a substitute teacher/tutor in elementary and middle schools, special education and a behavior interventionist for preschoolers with autism. In my opinion, mental health workers, clinicians, special education staff hold the space for the kids to grow up while they work and struggle within the family and legal systems that strive to protect minors.

In some circumstances it takes growing to adulthood to start to peel away at the process of taking responsibility for self. It may take longer for some of us to get there because the depth of betrayal to us as innocents is deeply rooted in our defense mechanisms. Sacred timing, solid intention, action and support with a heart for forgiveness and gratitude are essential to get the process started and eventually to completion.

Let's return to Mike who has at this point contacted a coach because he is tired of thinking ill of his co-workers and feeling left out. The coach points out that in Mike's recent history he has already resigned from the last two jobs. Not feeling the camaraderie with coworkers, Mike thought he did not have a good future with the previous companies. How many more times will Mike continue this trend?

Mike's coach, after asking some questions about experiences at work and in childhood, invites Mike to stand at the seven-year-old marker along the Time Circle and to find out from his inner seven-year-old what it was like for him in elementary school. What happened then that makes Mike feel left out now?

Mike, at this point, regrets his decision to hire the coach and explore. This is feeling very weird, and he finds that he is resisting the process. The coach reminds Mike that it is totally his choice and that this work can always be revisited. After imagining what his life might be like if he resigns from yet another company, Mike decides to "suck it up" and move forward despite feeling ridiculous.

Mike makes the first move to *Reclaim* this younger aspect of self. "Hey, little dude" says the adult Mike, feeling very awkward at first speaking to an imagined little self. "What's up?" Mike glances at his coach with eyes that relay how uncomfortable he is with this experience. The coach reminds him, with her eyes, that there is no judgement. It is totally up to Mike and what does he have to lose? What might he gain?

Mike exhales with lips pursed as if readying to lift heavy weights, "I wanted to check in because I had some coworkers not invite me to a dinner and it reminded me of when we were in school and often not chosen to join group games." "I want you to know that you are important and that I choose you to be on my team." "Is there anything you want from me?" Mike is getting warmed up.

How might the inner child respond to that? Perhaps there will be silence. Maybe, when the younger aspect of self is asked what he wants, and it is important to always check in and clarify, little Mike says that he wants present Mike to give him a "virtual" hug. Or maybe little Mike throws a big tantrum (for which present Mike experiences the emotions internally) and verbalizes his hurt and anger. With a little more probing, to communicate fully, clarify and be certain one has covered all bases, present Mike discovers how little Mike feared he was being judged by others. What did those elementary kids say to little Mike? What is Mike thinking his co-workers are saying about him now? What opinion did he form about himself at age seven and was it true? We wonder if present Mike still carries this belief about himself.

Little Mike expresses that he wants a hug because he has felt very alone. Present Mike is kneeling and wondering again why he agreed to this because he feels not just a little silly but rather utterly ridiculous. Despite his discomfort and feeling like he must try something to turn his life around, he bravely reaches his arms out to the "empty space" in front of him and embraces his inner seven-year-old.

Inside Mike's mind, he recalls images of little Mike alone in the school yard or hiding out in a classroom at recess. Mike's eyes are misted with tears and in his gut, he feels the importance of the "make believe" hug despite still feeling uncomfortable with the exchange overall. The coach asks Mike to tell the younger aspect what Mike wishes someone would have told him when he was seven years old.

With a deep hug he tells little Mike what he needed to have heard long ago and commences the process of *Reconciling* and *Reframing*: "You know little guy, what those kids said about you being slow and stupid?" "It was never true!" "There was never anything wrong with you!" Coach urges him to speak in the present: "There IS nothing wrong with you". "I love that you see things from a perspective that many other people do not see!" "And guess what?" "I am still someone who sees things differently from others which is something my co-workers appreciate about me."

Recalling the difficulty sitting still at his desk at school, present Mike adds, "Also, I have learned that I need to move around when I am working." "It is hard for me to sit still so I just get up and either walk around my office or use my balance board." Still embracing little Mike, present Mike's coach, kneeling at his side, encourages him, if it feels right, to take a deep breath to anchor the experience of the "embrace" in his body. Mike complies because the suggestion resonates, and he is glad that they are alone in a room where no one can see him.

Let's get back to the hug. Mike was ready then to place the inner seven-year-old directly into his heart, now *Reclaiming* a younger aspect of self and *Realigning* with the truth. At little Mike's request, he promises to listen to and take good loving care of his younger self. What does it mean to place the inner seven-year-old into Mike's heart? First – to place the younger aspect into one's heart is to (1) set the intention to do so and then (2) take the imaginary aspect of self, from the hug for example, and physically place one's hands from hug to heart, motioning receiving that aspect of self into their heart of Now.

What does it mean when Mike's younger self requests that present Mike "listen to and take good loving care of him"? Be sure of what you agree to. Ask for specifics! When little Mike was asked for an example of what it would look like for present Mike to "take good loving care" of him, little Mike gave the example of letting "him" use the balance board at work. Adult Mike agreed that he would specifically imagine little Mike on the balance board with him.

To this day, the smile on Mike's face when he steps onto that board is a delight to him. Each muscle twitch of striving balance is anchoring in the truth of the judgement from the past: little Mike and present Mike were not "slow and stupid." The truth is they prefer to think while in motion and like to see all the angles of a topic. They are blessed in being themselves, growing and learning along the way. Mike brought awareness and gratitude for his inner relationship with little Mike into his Now. Mike is doing better as he knows better.

If it was Mike's soul's curriculum to learn this lesson, chances are even if some fine loving adults had intervened on his behalf, it wouldn't have mattered. Sometimes, when the lesson is deeply needed, a child/person won't receive it until they have more experience. Have you ever had a child ask you for a cookie, for example, and you say yes, and then they start crying as if you had said no? Well, I have. In those cases, the psyche may have already scripted certain belief systems and they hear "no" despite the spoken "yes". "Take the cookie!" "Yes! You can eat the cookie!" in sacred timing, of course.

Little Mike may not have received the message earlier in life because he saw the world through the lens of his learning or rather, being denied a cookie because he was still limited by his belief system. He sensed he was being judged by his peers, and like many of us, part of him believed the nonsense was true. How might we be denying ourselves offered cookies in life these days after requesting them? Think about it. What's our sacred timing for taking the cookie when it is wanted and offered?

Furthermore, whether his colleagues consciously or unconsciously do not invite him to dinner is of no consequence. He recognizes the trigger and takes a few deep breaths while considering the truth. He may choose to reach out to a coworker for clarification on the invite list or let it go this time because he has reconciled within himself. Mike now also remembers how to take time during the day to "balance" and "play" which makes for a lighter perspective.

You Remember Gratitude Reality? Gratitude may be inherent in an occurrence or perhaps be discerned in retrospect. And sometimes, additional gratitude rises when the heart is more open and freed further into expanded awareness. While "visiting" with his inner seven-year-old, present Mike realizes that his second-grade teacher, Mr. Jenkins, really did see and support him. Mike used to think Mr. Jenkins thought he was kooky and wondered why the teacher bothered to talk to him.

While standing in silence, Mike recalls how Mr. Jenkins took the time to listen to seven-year-old Mike talk about dinosaurs and encouraged him to mimic how some of them moved their massive bodies. Mr.

Jenkins allowed Mike to "hide out" in his classroom during lunch and recess by keeping his door open for students to enter at will. Responding to his life coach's suggestion and with his younger self in his heart, present Mike takes a moment to speak to Mr. Jenkins and express gratitude despite the exasperated glance towards his coach who lifts her arms and mouths the words 'your choice'.

"Thank you, Mr. Jenkins for all the support you gave me. I didn't realize, until I looked back on those second-grade days, just how amazing you were to me." Suddenly, present Mike is overwhelmed by the emotions flowing with tears streaming down his face. This was the poignant point of deeper forgiveness. Sometimes gratitude triggers it. Trust the process.

Remembering all the lunchtimes he hid out in the classroom, how blessed he was that Mr. Jenkins was in his life at that time! When asked by his coach what was present for him after thanking Mr. Jenkins, Mike vows to take time in life to support others, at work or in his private life, as Mr. Jenkins had done for seven-year-old Mike. Mr. Jenkins didn't judge him as kooky; the truth was, seven-year-old Mike was simply being seen and he did not know how to assimilate it because he was so accustomed to being ridiculed by his peers.

The potential result of Mike's willingness to take the Peace on Purpose journey is that he will be an amazing father, uncle, friend, mentor, manager etc. should he choose to be. Also, he is well on his way to internalizing very loving parents, which in my opinion is the key to emotional maturity and a good life: to be guided by inner loving parents.

Mike's story is an example of how one may choose to circle back. Will the triggering scenario of fear of being left out and feeling rejected just disappear? Probably, as with an onion, layers will be peeled, and the subsequent times a similar situation occurs, present Mike will hold that inner child in his intention, and strip away more layers until one day, what used to be a triggering experience, becomes a simple response, a choice. Mike, moving forward may not notice anything amiss, whether invited to dine with his coworkers or not. If he chooses to ask for clarification, he will.

Being in the Now and physically walking the Time Circle to communicate with younger/older aspects of self (not speaking about them, but rather to them), sharing healing and gratitude, is the key to anchoring healing and aliveness into the body. Gratitude brings one into the Now, which to me is aliveness. Some people believe that this "true" healing is slated to be the kind that reaches back to the Ancestors and forward to posterity or to the lives one has yet to touch. From a scientific perspective we know at least that epigenetics, the expression of the gene sequence (not the DNA coding) of one's cells can be modified for the better.

I believe that true healing changes me for the better at the cellular level. The negative changes to my genetic expression, caused by the patterns of how I perceived and responded to my environment, can be modified. For example, post-traumatic stress (PTS) is shown to damage the DNA sequence. Patients who work on healing their PTS show positive reversible effects on their DNA sequence.

How do you want to affect the sequences in your life's expression? What reactions would you like to heal and convert into calm responses? I prefer to reconcile judgements and dissolve them into assessments. We talk "to" those parts of ourselves instead of "about" those parts of ourselves. Let the mind believe the healing for my inner seven-year-old is happening Now. *Well, it sort of is, isn't it?*

Mike Circles Forward to an Older Aspect of Self

As Mike and the coach briefed the session, they discussed the option of circling forward to speak to an elder self, or to receive messages from one's elder self. What if present thirty-year-old Mike Time Circled forward to connect with sixty-five-year-old Mike? What might the older adult self say to thirty-year-old Mike?

Are you wondering why Mike decided to circle forward to age sixty-five? We were thrilled for him when he completed the process earlier with the younger aspect of self and had worked out some impressions of his co-workers. Plus, he seemed so miserable and uncomfortable during the process, right?

After further discussion with his coach, Mike makes the choice to circle forward to connect with his future sixty-five-year-old self because he wants to imagine becoming someone who had committed to his life both professionally and personally. In a way, he wanted to "try on" how his life might be if he were no longer feeling "left out" and reacting to situations as he had in the past when he had quit several jobs. You go Mike!

Standing at the position of sixty-five on the circle, Mike looked at the thirty-year marker and laughed. Mike felt silly and excited doing this exercise. Have I not healed enough? "Geez!" "Why did I agree to this?" Mike whispered with a sigh. The coach smiled and reminded him that he had shared that he cannot picture his future. Mike chuckled to himself. He had set himself up!

The woman reiterated that it is his choice. Mike shuffled his feet as if to get a better feel for the ground at age sixty-five. He looked toward position thirty again, glanced up at the ceiling and closed his eyes. "Who am I?" he wondered for a moment.

Mike placed his hands together, in an almost prayer-like position and raised them toward his mouth as he exhaled into them. Thinking to himself "I already feel nuts, might as well go with it" he resigned himself and briefly closed his eyes. Opening his eyes and looking at the age thirty mark, he says to his younger self, "We have been pretty solid in life" "Been blessed with good jobs and enough money to get by and have some fun."

Opening himself to imagine a future, he adds, "More than that, my marriage is solid and a few really good grown-up kids also exist". "The younger one uses my balance board," he suddenly adds. "I am good with me, so I have managed to do okay with co-workers too through the years." "I don't sweat the small stuff and have settled into my job as a manager over the years."

Mike walks back to present age and looks at his coach. To her silence he comments "I still feel ridiculous." To her added silence he says, "And I feel solid." "Like I trust the more mature man in me." "Kind of like, I know he, or we, will figure out the answers."

That week Mike's team stopped off at Herman's Diner at the close of a case. There was one large pie for dessert left that the attendant brought over for the team to share. Mike was happy to be included. If he had looked a little closer, he would have noticed that not only was he included by the team, but he also felt belonging just being himself.

And What if Mike Didn't Circle Back?

How does the example of Mike circling back to his inner seven-year-old resonate for you? Let's imagine Mike refused to go back to seven-year-old Mike after he consciously or unconsciously identified the trigger. Let's consider what Mike's experience might have been if he had not circled back. What would have been a likely outcome?

1. Mike could build resentment towards his team, maybe never even inquire as to why he did not receive an invitation to

dinner.

2. That resentment might cause Mike to overtly or covertly refuse to help colleagues in the office when asked and/or withhold when he knew that he could be helpful.

3. Mike may begin to see false patterns in his interoffice relations imagining that most transactions are due to others not including him on purpose.

Simply put, Mike would become an office victim or possibly an office jerk. Jennifer Thompson has a pivotal book for the corporate world entitled "Martyrs, Victims & Jerks" in the workplace. If Mike did not Time Circle his story and begin to bridge the healing between himself and his inner seven-year-old, let's face it, he would be on the road to becoming a victim or jerk.

Even if he asked for clarification without using the Time Circle, would he believe that his colleagues innocently forgot? Instead, becoming a victim his thoughts might be: "No one likes me!" "They didn't invite me to the after work gathering!" Another angle might be Mike responding in an "I'll show them" manner and become a real jerk in his work behavior. Our Mike could end up as a martyr, victim or jerk at work!

These potential behaviors would result in Mike not including teammates. Mike would be doing to them, what he judged they were doing to him. Check out Jennifer Thompson's book "Martyrs, Victims & Jerks" NoMVJ.com and the services of Silverstrandgroup.com. Its wisdom will cultivate your self-awareness and work life for the better!

What is our response to Mike's process around the Time Circle? As we read the story of Mike's Peace on Purpose journey, we may notice parts of ourselves revealing the first clue about "where" we should begin should we choose to embark on this journey.

The thing is WE already know where those pieces are in ourselves that we want to retrieve and/or thank. I believe that everyone has their own wisdom inside of them to choose to access or not to access. I had wonderful instructors at the University of Santa Monica, Counseling and Spiritual Psychology programs, and Women Within Int'l programs who taught me again and again that I have my own answers inside of me, that I am exactly where I need to be on my journey, that growth is a process and (I will add via Maya Angelou) as I know better, I do better.

Thank you, "Mike" for the courage to share your story and assisting us in potentially receiving insight through your strength of heart.

Chapter 4

The Four Directions and Gratitude of the Time Circle

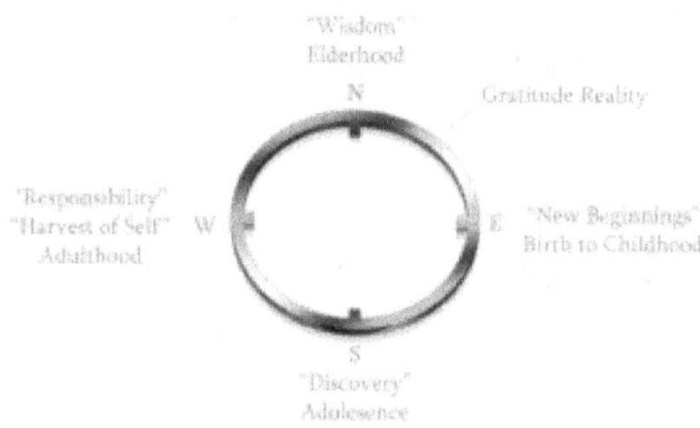

The East – Birth – New Beginnings

The east is Birth and childhood. It represents new beginnings. The section that covers east to south represents birth to the start of adolescence. This period is packed with developmental stages in human life.

Infancy represents Trust vs. Mistrust: HOPE

Toddler months are Autonomy vs Shame/Doubt: WILL POWER

Three years old to six years old is Initiative vs Guilt: PURPOSE

Six years old to eleven years old is Industry vs. Inferiority: COMPETENCE

As I travel from east to the south, chronologically, I cover four life stages. There is no need to overly focus on the meaning of each stage. The stages are mentioned as a point of reference to inspire recall. It is important for us to get more deeply in touch with ourselves during the time period represented. What do our younger selves have to say?

When teaching others about the East Stage of the circle I ask participants to picture a four-year-old, practicing cartwheels. Question: What if the four-year-old is doing cartwheels and no one around says anything about the cartwheels to that child? What does a kid do or say when they are trying to get our attention? "Watch this" they may command ad nauseam. They are relentless in getting what they want! And good for them because what they want is so much more than us simply watching them do the cartwheel – they want a positive, or a realistic reflection of self that is connected to us so they can in turn connect to self. They want to feel seen. "Look at me! Look at me!" demands the four-year-old.

I like to ask clients "How does the four-year-old feel if people are there, but no one is watching and/or commenting?" Typically, they suggest that maybe the kid felt sad or mad. Maybe they felt like they weren't good enough or worthy enough even if they couldn't articulate their feelings at such a young age.

Then I would ask the clients for ideas on what the adults around the young cart wheeler "should have" said to them. "Good job!" "Nice cartwheel!" The kid's inner response to that type of praise might be "Oh! So, you like my cartwheels!" "I am going to keep doing 'good' ones then so I can get attention from you!" They might feel pressure, "I hope I can keep doing 'good' cartwheels."

The alternative meaning is that if their cartwheels are not good, do they deserve the attention? Are they inherently worthy of our gaze? And let's face it, at this point most of us hear crickets or we are told by loved ones that we are amazing, even if our cartwheels are not, until the reality of being assessed by someone like Simon Cowell of America's Got Talent occurs in life. Quite a rude awakening!

Unless one has agreed to a gymnastic competitive event for which they are training, does it matter if they technically executed a "good" or "bad" cartwheel? They are four years old and not trying out for the Olympics! Imagine if the cartwheel wasn't qualified as positive or negative. Can't it just have been a cartwheel? An effort? "I see you doing cartwheels!" "You are making the effort!" "I see you on your hands, with your legs flying over your head."

What if the little one receives praise – not for doing a "good" cartwheel, but rather for making the effort to do the cartwheel? "I see you doing cartwheels!" The purpose becomes the effort instead of the qualification of "good" or "bad" as deemed by someone else. They want to be seen, just for being.

Consider a few different lines of self-talk running through their mind with each of the two scenarios. One is subconsciously or consciously trying to define what "good" means – again, this is not an event tryout – there is no major rubric to follow. They are four years old goofing around on the lawn. Feeling anxious they might wonder, "What if now I do a 'bad' cartwheel?!" How might that four-year-old feel now with such thoughts? What if they execute a "good" cartwheel, but the adult was checking their phone when they did it and they didn't say anything to the kid?

Now the four-year-old might think the cartwheel wasn't good enough or maybe that they are not good enough. Of course, the adult could just ask the child what they thought about their own cartwheel too! Most adults don't empower young kids that much and maybe the trend is changing with the newer generations.

In any event, without an assist with empowering self-assessment by the four-year-old, they are more likely to set themself up to compete with others before they have been able to establish a rubric of learning for themselves. They will compare their value to their idea of the worth of others. "Look at me! Look at me!" potentially a set up for a "sore loser" or "sore winner".

The second line of script that could germinate in the four-year-old is a clean line of simply being visible and seen - I am seen making an effort and my subconscious response to this might be "I am seen", "I am going to do another cartwheel". This sets them up to initially be a competitor within self, striving for their personal level of excellence before ever concerning themself about competing with others.

Instead of qualifying this version as "the winner" or "the good" one, let's instead give it a birthing rating, for example from 1-10 centimeters on the way to being born. Why look at it this way? Because growth is a process, not an event! Thank you USM for grounding that learning into me.

If they get through the stage feeling seen, and in this case, autonomous, that was a 10-centimeter birthing! Sounds silly, doesn't it? And are you beginning to sense just how often people are qualifying outcomes as "good" or "bad"? "Low functioning" or "high functioning"? It's okay to qualify – and how would our lives be different if we had been free from it while we were developing our sense of self, at least in the formative years?

If I could develop as a person before facing a sea of qualifiers? I understand the need to qualify for many thought processes and assessments, and I am also very aware of the effects premature qualification may have on one's formative years.

How might life be different, if while I was establishing my sense of true self, I could stand on foundations of completing life growth stages with self-awareness and confidence before comparing my "skills" with those of other people? I believe I would have gained a solid sense of self, enough so that when comparing myself to others, the potential disparity would not include the value of self; not mine or theirs.

To develop through a formative life stage without qualifying the value of the effort, for example, ideally, the four-year-old cart wheeler will feel seen for their unique striving. They might also learn about the cartwheel rubric so to decide if honing the cartwheel skill might be a goal that they have. Picture that meeting with a gymnastic judge in the future to assess the cartwheel. The gist is, if one gets a poor score on the cartwheel rubric it does not correlate to one's inherent value.

This is tricky to self-navigate, and as an adult on the scene, I certainly want my input to assist minors in developing a hardy sense of self-worth along with an understanding of the steps needed and further effort required to technically improve a cartwheel, for example. If as an adult I can help illuminate a minor's awareness of appreciation for their efforts and inherent sense of self? Invaluable.

Some of us only develop a permeable path so that all or most external feedback becomes a barometer of self-worth. First, I want to internalize feeling seen for effort, because I am enough. Then I can grapple with my cartwheel scores. The main branch on our tree of life, the rooted trunk, is our self-worth. There are plenty of limbs and branches through life's seasons for cartwheels, debate teams, basketball, singing lessons, and other expressions down the line. The foundation, however, is critical.

Why circle back to scan past events? Ever return as an adult to places of your childhood? Often the ways a child recalls events and people are skewed from the adult view of the situation in retrospect. Therefore, it is important, should we notice something out of sync, in my opinion, to occasionally "scan" our past, through the present "I know better" perspective, to determine if we left some major unfinished business that is causing upheaval in the present. Basically, it is like a visual sweep of our lives from the present view as we step across the Bridge of Curiosity. Get some popcorn ready as we sit back and scan the life stages!

Let's imagine that overall, the four-year-old didn't receive a connected reflection. Instead, maybe no one commented much at all as they attempted cartwheels. "Look at me!" "Look at me!" They continued to chant as they got older because perhaps, they only managed to be reconciled to 6 centimeters birthing and are moving on to the next life stage with a development aspect that is stunted, "mid birthing."

Becoming an adolescent, they stand at the south of the circle.... What might happen next to a youngster entering adolescence when their inner "cartwheeling" 4-year-old still feels unseen, was stunted at 6 centimeters birthing and is now in a 15-year-old body?

The South – Adolescence- Discovery

During adolescence one can become cognizant of the inner script being written or the "self-talk". How do I measure up amongst my peer group, leaders and organizations with which I am involved? Adolescence is a time of discovery.

Do you remember high school? What was that time of life like for you? I recall being called a "biatch". A loner. A lonely "biatch" or angry "biatch". I was in an all-girl catholic school, and I pushed the limits with all due respect. For example, I was forced to attend chapel on first Fridays. I refused to pray unless I felt like praying, which I calmly communicated to the nuns as I smoldered internally. "You can force me to sit in chapel," "but you cannot force me to pray!" That was my mantra. What could they do? I was serious too! If I felt like "praying" the way I had been conditioned, I did. Sometimes, I prayed my own way, in silence, attempting to commune with something much more aligned to me than the religion that was being taught to me.

Prayer was a personal experience for me; not one that could be regurgitated at the sound of a bell. My friends and I had no problem with Jesus. It was the lack of equal rights, money that could be used to revamp systems to help the starving and homeless and our judgement of the limiting beliefs the church represented, that we could have done without.

I believe in the power of Jesus and other amazing beings who have walked the Earth. Sometimes I can still choose an empty church, in lieu of nature to commune with "Spirit" because the energy present is sacred and peaceful. I refuse to place a cap on the potential wisdom sources and in doing so, I truly do not mean to insult anyone's heart of beliefs. With me, there is room for all that is Light. To argue would be me busy being "right." I much prefer curiosity.

I was miserable in high school. I moved out of the Bronx to Westchester County, New York and was new to the area. My parents had me choose between the local public high school or the catholic all girls. I really had wanted co-ed, but I hung out with some kids from the local public high school at my parents' golf club. I knew they cut class and further, I knew myself well enough to know that if it were easy to cut class, I would too. Why? Because then I could smoke cigarettes, which was a major activity in my life for many years.

I chose the catholic school which was my dramatic misery for four years because I wanted to support myself in getting into college. Yay me! That was an early lesson in blame because I couldn't blame my parents. They let me choose. Well-played, mom and dad! And it turned out okay. I survived by laughing with some wonderful people. I had good friends who found ways to spread creative mischief and we got through it.

How about you? What names were you called in high school? What names did you bestow on others? How were you treated by peers and how did you treat yourself? Did you believe what was said about you? I internalized being called an angry and lonely "biatch" for years. I think it was partially true. I was harsh, even crude at times. I was very out of touch with how sacred and precious I was in my body. I felt my spirit but wasn't really in my body. I smoked at least a pack of cigarettes a day and didn't know how to express my emotions constructively.

Let's review the life stages of adolescence. The main stage is Identity versus Role Confusion which adjusts to FIDELITY. Becoming faithful to myself in identifying and expressing who I am is the goal. Teenagers are figuring out who they are. They are gaining awareness of the words they want written as part of their script in life, so to speak. The question is do they persist in allowing themselves to author their script or with role confusion, do they also take on the words and ways of others and make them their inauthentic own? As they figure out how to authentically produce their voice and way of being they are becoming faithful to themselves as they allow the process to unfold.

There is also another stage that is technically part of adulthood and I think may easily begin in late adolescence which is Intimacy versus Isolation. Intimacy versus Isolation with the goal being LOVE. Learning true intimacy is to first know self. Without knowing self or still at the early stages of figuring ourselves out, we may be more inclined to seek ourselves in others. In seeking our reflection in others, we generally use sex as a way of getting closer to them or to ourselves.

As the goal of LOVE is being realized, it is the potential onset of self-love which in turn gets reflected out as love of and for others with connected intimacy of communication and awareness. As we rescript our stories, removing what was imposed upon us, like the names we were called in high school, and begin to replace the old script with the first of many versions of the truth script, what we believe to be true about ourselves emerges. We work towards illuminating LOVE. This is a sacred process, often with many discoverable layers.

LOVE and FIDELITY. By the time I was seventeen I was so sick of hearing friends describe how in love they were with their boyfriends – their "first" lover etc. I vowed not to be chained to the experience and ending up struggling to move on from my "first" love all because of the additional emotional attachment.

I decided to make sure that my "first" was not someone I loved. Does this sound like a good strategy to you? Me neither. That was the disconnect for me because I was not yet intimate with myself. It took me many, many years to learn to be faithful to myself. I said previously that I thought angry/lonely biatch was partially true. I believed it. I was isolated within myself, an aspect of me that took some time to unravel over the years so I could live from a different script.

Now, how about that four-year-old who did the cartwheels? "Look at me!", "Look at me!" How are they doing in high school? What might they want you to notice about them now? Maybe it is "Look at me!" "I have a great body!" "Look at me!" "I have an expensive car!" "I have blue hair!" etc. What do we really want in those years? We want intimacy and somehow most of us think intimacy is sex, when sex is really more of an expressive byproduct of someone who knows how to be intimate, connected with themself and then with a specific someone.

Initially, intimacy refers more to basic connection, communication and understanding of self and other. To be intimate is also to feel seen and understood. It is knowing not to compromise self in order to feel loved. Sexual intimacy can be a choice, ideally, following deeper interconnectedness. Sadly, growing up, many of us mistakenly think that sex or love making will result in foundational connection. Does it?

There are self-connected people who have sex simply because they wish to. I think someone can be intimate with themself enough to know that they want to go have sex with someone, even if randomly. And I trust the lessons we are all here to learn to some extent.

In short, it's none of my business. Random sex isn't really my way because my sex life started off as a bit random. I want connection and congruency all around. I am particular about who gets to experience that part of me. I am lucky that I found me after I fought to find myself. I prefer to have that sentiment be mutual and specific. I have waited alone for years to make up for lost time.

Back to the name calling. Some teens are called boy toy, jock, nerd, players, druggies, whores, skanks, biatches, goths, "dickheads", "pussies" etc. The sentiment stays the same though some of the terms change through the years. And while we are on the topic, why do we use slang names of our body parts to insult each other? And how did the term pussy ever evolve to mean weak? None of us would be alive if vaginas were weak! I have three kids. You give birth or pull a Cornish game hen through your nostril three times and then dare to say any vagina is weak! And what inspired the term dickhead? There is an interesting story there and no reason to treat our sacred body parts this way.

In high school, many of us take on those names like skinny jeans at the mall. They become part of our identities, and the dye might seep into our bloodstreams just enough to take hold. Who were we in high school? Are we who "they" said we were? Well, that is the thing. It really is up to us to decide who we are and to what and to whom we want to ascribe our LOVE and FIDELITY.

How do we decide? Hopefully, we have some support from very wise people who can truly reflect to us that they see the effort of our "cartwheels". If we are luckier, we already see that we are sacred. It is more than likely that we are struggling to find our sacred selves. "Look at me!" "I got into the best college!" "Better than yours!", "Look at me!" "I made thousands of dollars selling drugs!"

Let's face it. If we are still in the "Look at me" stage, we likely have not grasped the idea of intimacy with self or others in terms of communication, connection, clarification and potentially sexually. Therefore, we are not that present to who we are as evidenced by superficially comparing ourselves to others.

Me? In high school I had taken the skills of angry and lonely biatch and vowed to become a lawyer to fight the catholic church on abortion. Not because I wanted to see more abortions in the world, but because I wanted people to be able to choose not to have one. I hated that the nuns would debate this with us. I very nicely accused them of not thinking for themselves. They had to spew the doctrine, therefore, to me, they were not reliable expert witnesses. They spoke for the hive, said angry biatch.

The truth was that they spoke their sacred beliefs and there was nothing wrong with that. Yes. I was a pain in the butt. In a good way. I am sure they prayed for me. Looking back, I do appreciate that very much.

And the people in high school who we made fun of? I will speak for me: they were probably way ahead of me in terms of self-awareness and self-sacredness. They made different choices than I did. It doesn't mean their lives were better or worse than mine. I trust that their lives were on curriculum with their learning. All their life puzzle pieces fit together congruently long before I figured out it could be otherwise.

So where was I leaving high school as I was moving on to the next life stage of Adulthood? I had not completed growing in the Adolescent stage. On the birthing centimeter scale of those formative years, I was stuck ramming my head against the pubic bone of life at a solid seven centimeters. Stuck and couldn't see it! I felt I was from another planet and still searching for my people in life. Still searching for myself.

So, what did I care? As long as there weren't any "no smoking" signs, I could wait it out with a pack of cigarettes. Plus, it gave me time to be uncomfortable which ultimately aided and abetted my self-understanding. How else would I ever get to adulthood?

The West - Adulthood

The west is the responsibility that comes with adulthood. I like to think of it as the time of the Harvest of the Self. At the beginning of adulthood there is some carryover from the adolescent development stage—Intimacy vs Isolation, which strives to adjust to LOVE. One may be learning how to be intimate with self and others. It is very likely that as we enter adulthood, we're still figuring out who we are and who we want to be.

The adult stage is Generativity versus Self-Absorption, which adjusts to CARE. Generativity is engaging in acts to promote the wellbeing of younger generations. My own experience of the adult stage is that there is a wide array of awareness from one's early twenties to early retirement years. Me? I knew everything when I was twenty. Pretty much knew everything other than how to truly CARE for myself. I had it all figured out!

So, what happened to the "cartwheeler" in adulthood? They may be saying "Look at me! I have the best job", "the most expensive house," etc. "I got the promotion!" Alternatively, they could be proclaiming "Look at me." "I got passed up for the promotion again." "Look at me." "I am a failure." "I am struggling to get through each day."

When does it end? Sounds exhausting, doesn't it? And the struggles are very real. They take their toll on people. I wish I had a magic wand to remove everyone's pain and misfortune. From what I have gathered thus far, life on Earth involves some amount of suffering. I am not sure there is any way around it. The way seems to be to get through it, learn the lesson, share forgiveness, embrace gratitude and just keep going.

When I became an adult, I was on the journey towards generativity, while still learning how to care for myself and others. The journey involved healing as much of me as possible, taking responsibility for pain, blame and embracing gratitude. Remember the first chapter "Considerations for the Journey", the section about judgement versus assessment? We explored the belief that the emotions of judgement usually point to some unfinished business in the person holding the judgment.

In my twenties I started having "reactions" when I heard that someone had a baby, and they were "disappointed" that it wasn't a boy or a girl etc. I didn't fully understand it at the time but those "reactions" were the reason I never found out the sex of my kids when I was pregnant. Also, gender means very little to me. Having a boy does not guarantee fulfillment of some archaic definition of what it means to be "male." Thankfully evolution has way more in store for us than the typical and limited expectations and definitions of the past. Things are changing with the newer generations.

The emotional reaction I had towards people expressing disappointment about the sex of their children directed me to look deeper. I focused some of my personal growth work on discovering why I was blaming people, judging them as dishonoring their babies. I was really angry.

As I took responsibility for my anger and explored the pattern of reaction, I discovered a path that took me back to my birth. I faced this work when I was at Woman Within, in my early thirties and followed up for another layer of healing at USM.

I was the third daughter in an Italian American family. There was a strong possibility that I was born into disappointment. Even if only for ten minutes? Very high likelihood! Additionally, I realized that growing up I had also tried to be "tough" and less "feminine" too. Nothing wrong with being less feminine regardless of how it is defined, my point is that I was denying myself expression on purpose. I wanted to be a son too, or at least my idea of what "son" would look like. Somewhere in my psyche was the experience that my parents were crestfallen because I was female.

If you recall from the Foreword, my grandmother anchored in me seeds of belonging. "The boy wasn't meant to be," "You, Giulia." "You were meant to be." Thank you, grandma. Thank you! I cannot imagine how I would have felt in my early thirties figuring out the obvious if she had not already germinated fierce love in me.

Were my parents doing their best? Yes! There was no ill intention. And since they didn't know how to pull the disappointment out of my aura, so to speak, or even know that it was there, life carried on. I was loved and there was a preverbal pain I could not pinpoint for years. Once I understood the connection between me judging new parents for being let down by the "gender" of their newborn and the personal pain in me, I went after the healing of it.

As an adult, it was my responsibility to go back to my birth and fawn over luminous me. I chose to follow through instead of blaming others. I did use the opportunity to step back along the Time Circle to meet me at birth. I sure was glowing as a newborn! In fact, I shone with sacred, sacred presence at birth. I was precious. I am precious and sacred even now.

I chose this family, DNA and logistics so I could learn the specific curriculum my soul needs to advance. Advance to where? I say to "somewhere." For now, I am right here. Right now. Sacred. Precious. I am grateful to have this healing around my birth story.

At the onset of adulthood, we can align with the Harvest of Self. We can rescript all the "stuff" we had been running in our minds rather unconsciously for years and begin to decide for ourselves. Hopefully with the assistance of some wise elders, we will decide who we are in the world and how we want to express aliveness in terms of work, family, hobbies, volunteering etc. What legacies do we want to leave in the wake of our life?

At the Harvest, we get to become acquainted with the blessings we have to offer to the world. Does that mean our names will be up in lights and we will be famous or infamous? Not necessarily. Sharing our gifts with the world does not equate to being a celebrity. We can, however, be shining stars of aliveness, as loving and wise mentors for self and others.

The process of meeting the self takes place many times over if one is paying attention. As we grow, we get to rescript and organize our inner and outer direction in life. I went from wanting to attend law school to going to massage school and then later to completing an MA in Spiritual Psychology and Counseling. I was still changing and growing way into adulthood. I wonder if my husband would have married me had he prior knowledge of the altered decisions I would make. Maybe we both imagined something or someone different? I wasn't fully formed, and he perhaps had signed up for "someone else."

Growth often brings change. Apparently, I had signed up to strive for the All of me! I am so glad that I did. The more I get to know me, the more I love me and realize that there is so much to learn. By the "All" of me I mean that I asked the Universe to help me grow to my fullest potential in this life. Seemed like a good idea at the time. Life has brought me some interesting twists and turns. Learning is not always fun as it is occurring. I am still on the path of learning and striving.

What are the blessings each of us offer and how do we want to express those blessings in life? In career and relationships? We harvest the self, each year. We pay attention to how the crops are faring because we want to be ready to provide them with a path to enough light should they by chance begin to grow alongside the shadow of a wall. As we know better, we do better. The beauty of the Harvest is that we can take the time to change direction, continually edit the script as we grow and as needed. The walk along the Time Circle offers the opportunity to "scan" certain experiences in our lives. The importance of scanning the Time Circle is to identify areas where we would benefit from healing and deepening gratitude.

Healing allows us to rescript our story, revising it to reflect the truth of who we are and who we want to be. If we heal through our hearts, then that shift anchors in, body, mind and heart. Hopefully, we exercise the right to do just that. Otherwise, we may choose to marinate on a throne of potential "fertilizer" otherwise known as B.S. or malarkey, for a while or maybe forever. We all have the proclivity to sit on a pile of our own "stuff" and stagnate. Moving forward is a matter of how to be and sacred timing.

At the time of this writing, I am standing at the fifty-seven-year-old mark around the Time Circle. I am getting more in sync with myself to some degree. I am still adjusting Generativity versus Self-Absorption to arrive at more CARE. I am walking around the Time Circle, scanning, to check in with myself.

My heart is full of the impact of the passing of my father and the culmination of the years of change since leaving my marriage, and subsequently my job in Los Angeles. I am surprised by the impasse in which I find myself. It is a much deeper experience than I had sensed was coming. I am aware of myself and making decisions for my future, one in which I mostly only take care of me. I must be able to stand on my own, so I do not walk into any more cages in my life and lock the gates.

My dad used to say "It's all B.S." when referring to life's happenings. Basically, a don't sweat the small stuff attitude. I agreed with him and would repeat it back to him until my early thirties and we would laugh together. Through personal growth education, when I realized that I could use all that B.S. or "stuff" to fertilize a new path for myself through responsibility and forgiveness my response to him changed.

I greatly desired to lighten the load I was carrying. The banter with my dad was so simple and fun that now that he is gone, I realize just how deeply this fertilizer is transforming my heart. Even though I am still adjusting to greater Generativity and CARE in this life stage of Adulthood, I feel more alive than ever.

I check in with myself around the Time Circle as I scan. Despite the fears that manage to reach my thoughts, I feel a deep surrender at this junction of my life. I am at a crossroads and find myself somewhat moving forward, because I know I am not stagnating. And yet, I am not covering much ground externally. I feel vulnerable and empowered all at the same time. What part of me do I speak to about this?

It was my dad's first birthday since his passing, and I was especially missing him. I looked out the window at the sea. I heard seagulls beckoning with their voices as they flew by. When I reflected on where at the Time Circle I should stand, I felt it was me in the present. As I acknowledged that, I had an image of Omak, the wolf with whom I was completely in sync. The love of my life! I looked deeper.

I recalled a photo I had of Omak lying on his back at my feet, offering me his belly. The immense power of leader energy, belly exposed, reveals confidence in vulnerability. I am certain that this is some of the most exquisite love in this world. So, why was I starting to sob? I was present and feeling. I was feeling the vulnerability of love and life at a much deeper level than I had previously allowed. It was all going through my heart. I thought about my dad telling me *it's all B.S.* I sensed his hand in sending feminine essence – in opening me to be willing to receive like Omak presenting for a belly rub. I was so grateful for this image and gift. Why did I feel a feminine essence coming to me? Because I was allowing myself to *receive*. Because I spent so many years trying to be "tough;" more inclined to give than to receive. What I am sharing has little to do with gender. It is about Essence.

It was as if the years I had spent inviting the feminine essence back to me, as it trickled in had been up leveled as the bulk of that part of me arrived. I revisited forgiveness. I forgave myself for ever having judged myself as less than for having been born female gender. I forgave myself for dishonoring myself. I know I was doing the best I could. I forgave myself for taking my feminine essence or rather my authentic essence and shoving it aside to be more "male," a son.

Even now, I continue to forgive myself for closing off part of my heart. Part of the sacred me and leaving it in shadow. I am receiving the softness of me. I am luminous, like I was at birth, shining feminine and masculine, both or neither. I am both bold color and soft light. I can be a warrior raising a sword and rock a baby to sleep – same as anyone else of any gender or essence. I can growl or purr with ease.

My heart has been raging with fierce love. I forgave myself for ever imagining that my father was disappointed in me being female. He may have longed for a son, and he was not disappointed in me. And you know what? Despite the unresolved logistical issues in my life, I also am not disappointed in me. In fact, I whole-heartedly approve of me and love me. I am with myself for the long haul.

I realized then that in order to complete this book so that I can be more generative or as generative as possible, this piece had to return to me. I welcome this essence home. I care for myself and this world. I want to give as much as I can for the betterment of all to the best of my ability. And I still have so much more to learn, to receive and to give.

This adult stage of the west is Generativity versus Self-Absorption which adjusts to CARE. I am taking the time to learn how to care for me, so I can be generative and care for others. I want to serve and give back to younger generations. I want to learn from the younger generations too.

How about us? No matter how old we are now, what do we care about in this world? How will the world, any part of it regardless of scope, be better because we were here? Even if we are in our early twenties, we can impact the younger generation by how we choose to be. And if we were to imagine ourselves at eighty years old, what legacy do we want to leave behind via our intention? How are we expressing purpose? Peacefully purposeful steps? Cartwheels?

Speaking of which... How about our cartwheeling friend? Let's check in!

The North – Elderhood

The north is the place of the elder, where wisdom resides. Where Integrity versus Despair adjusts amongst "mankind" versus "my kind" with WISDOM as the goal. To me, it is the place where the wind dances and the stars are revealed in the sky like an army of Ancestral Guides at our service. How do we want them to assist?

After we have harvested the self for many years, we hope to be well on our way to thinking about others. If we are not all wrapped up in our woes, we are more inclined to see the world with our hearts. In short, the questions are: How are we now as elders? How do we want to be if we get to be "old"?

Let's take our cartwheeling friend. They are now eighty years old and still saying "Look at me!" "My son bought me a new couch!" or "Look at me!" "I have cancer again." "Look! My grandchildren won all the most prestigious awards!" Look at them – on the surface of life, they have checked all the boxes created by some entity that set the "standard" called the Jones'.

They worked hard to keep up with the Jones' and to do what they thought was "right." Are they deeply happy with their choices? Proud for persevering? Are they happy beyond whether or not they managed to check the boxes? If they define a life well lived mostly on what appears on the surface of life, without embracing gratitude and taking responsibility for blame, and pain, then there is a high likelihood that they continue to turn the spotlight on themselves. "Look at me!" Humankind versus my kind adjusts to WISDOM. In my opinion, the truth of wisdom is expanding to embracing "all kinds."

Take a few breaths and pause a moment. No matter what our chronological age may be today, how are we experiencing Wisdom in life?

Pause and breathe.

How do we rate our need to be in the spotlight?

Pause and breathe.

How do we rate our proclivity to shine the spotlight so to assist others?

We pause and breathe to maintain self-awareness. It is imperative that we persist in our growth so we may be of service to self and others. We continue to walk the Time Circle and scan memories and present intentions to do our best to express gratitude and take responsibility for pain and blame.

For me, I know my goal with respect to Wisdom. Long before I reach the age of eighty years my wisdom says that instead of "Look at me!", I want to be saying these words: **Look at all of you! How can I be of service to you?** I want to be of service and do not need accolades for that.

I can ask to be of service to others if I have already figured out how to be of service to myself or at least am actively working on it. This is the perspective that allows for gratitude to become a torus in one's heart. A torus that can link to all the grateful hearts of the world because it is its own language. In sacred geometry, a torus represents a continuous cycle of energy flowing in the Universe; all things interconnected.

Imagine this level of healing within one human being at a time. With all their trials, joys, tribulations, learnings, poignant and tear-filled forgivenesses through "life". This healing is a process, not an event! The way I see things, there is the "me" torus; the microcosm. There are the "us" toruses which expand to the macrocosm. I want to put my best torus forward! There is always more.

Some may think my thoughts about healing to be farfetched. Do you really think this is the first time someone has thought I was "kooky" in my life? Get to the back of the line and I will offer you a hug and look you in the eye when your turn comes. Why? Because I have lived long enough to know that every bad dream or "failure" or time someone didn't believe in me, or I didn't believe in myself was a challenge no matter how deflated I may have felt at the time.

At a young age I decided that the challenges meant that "I was on the rise" and imagined that something wanted to keep me from growing. At least that was the perspective of the angry teenager in me. Hey, I used whatever wisdom I had handy and that worked for me. The anger kept me in fight mode so I wouldn't give up and cave in on myself and it served me in those days.

The thing is that even though the "Elderhood" stage is for old age according to Eric Erickson's Life Stages, there is no reason a young person cannot already be operating from the spirit of "how can I be of service to all of you?" as they are also growing themselves.

Everyone has their own answers and wisdom inside of themselves. Of course, there are times when someone might have to rely on another person for guidance. What I am sharing relates to an age-appropriate healthy range of personal agency. There are circumstances where others may directly support a person's healing because that person is temporarily lost or is a danger to themselves or to others. I am advocating stretching for age-appropriate personal responsibility for those who have "healthy" agency.

The Peace on Purpose process is not easy. We may want to give up many times. Many times. We are still here, plugging away and following our wisdom as we continue to peel away at the layers of healing. Of course, we can choose to rest on the throne of limiting beliefs when needed too.

I sense that as I write this book, I am at the precipice of living my unknown dreams. To courageously walk towards unknown dreams because at this point, I have very little to lose and everything to gain and therefore more to receive and to give. I love the E.E. Cummings quote *It takes courage to grow up and become who you really are.* We are the light on the path of courage. We are not giving up. We are opening up.

When scanning the Time Circle, if we find ourselves in shadow, we keep moving. There is always more processing to be done! A line from one of my poems: "I am dancing with my shadow, gliding gracefully into the conscious dawn." Who better knows our old, patterned choreography than our shadow? The question is which part of us leads the dance? Us or shadow? We lead with illuminated healing, and we choose the destination to be the conscious dawn. This is symbolic of a sacred dance and partnership within us.

From the perspective of the north, I can look ahead at the ninety-year-old me. Did she see me through? I stand further ahead along the Time Circle taking my position at the ninety-year-old mark. I am amazed at how quickly and lightly I walk to the position. I look back toward fifty-seven-year-old me. My ninety-year-old face is smiling with eyes glistening. "You are dedicated to your soul's learning despite the frustration and hardships. You are true to yourself; doing your best to see with gratitude," she tells me with lightness to her voice.

Standing back at the fifty-seven-year-old mark I look forward again to age ninety. I still see the smiling face and I daresay she is laughing! Not laughing at me. She is free to laugh and shed tears. I find myself feeling excited to be further embraced by life as I move forward. Tears amidst the light of laughter? Tears of joy and compassion. I am a torus of letting go and receiving. Flow! I see how all my life came together thus far- and is coming together – all the "mistakes" that brought me the opportunity to learn or made it possible for my path to cross more easily with another person's path etc.

I see the blessings in what I have learned. We see the blessings in what we have learned. We keep going. We know better and we are choosing to do better and be better. Therefore, we know that we have the capacity to see gratitude and blessings amidst the baloney. There is truly so much for which we can be grateful! We see the fertilizing potential. Peace starts with us.

And our eighty-year-old cartwheeling friend? It is never too late to switch out a puzzle piece with its congruent counterpart. If we were to accompany the cartwheeler around the Time Circle back to that early developmental stage to support their intention to explore and to be seen with us as the witness, how would we support them?

Pay attention to me, the unacknowledged cartwheeler pleads. They spent much of their life working so hard to either check all the "right" boxes or at least to communicate their woes. "Look at me!!" How does someone carrying so many years of memories and potentially unreconciled blame and pain take to this book? To that we say that sacred timing is everyone's right. Do we think they are too old to heal? Do we believe that "old" dogs can learn new tricks?

My dad lived 91 years and navigated an Apple computer, iPhone and hearing aids with Bluetooth functionality. When my mom spoke, he sometimes increased the volume of his favorite orchestral "Victory at Sea" and smiled trying to annoy her purposefully which made him laugh, nodding his head while she talked. New tricks! We believe old dogs CAN learn new tricks. And what about people who act like lone wolves? Well, there is no such thing as a lone wolf. A wolf traveling alone is generally searching for its pack or mate, for something. Choose to grow or not to grow. No need to make excuses.

It is not for me to judge when or if a person should or should not heal. Not my business. I do know that the human spirit can move beyond shame, pain, regret, at any age. If there is a will to heal and face one's truth, the power of that healing will flood on through no matter how many years or decisions have passed.

Mourning a milestone through forgiveness will lead to a Morning Milestone; a new day. Chances are that the person will feel a great weight has been lifted even if life on the surface is not what they want. They may have regrets, and who doesn't at times? Well, those can be walked through the Peace on Purpose circle too, in sacred timing.

The "Look at me" eighty-year-old cartwheeler has made their way back around the Time Circle. Perhaps we watch them reclaim, reframe, reconcile and realign with aspects from their adulthood, adolescence and childhood. We are doing great in showing up as calm and respectful witnesses!

We come to the original "cartwheel" event in their life. The precious four-year-old, eager to feel seen. We are privileged to witness the eighty-year-old cartwheeler see their precious four-year-old self. "What do you want from me precious one?" the elder asks their younger self. In response they hear "Watch this!" The elder smiles as they envision themself doing cartwheels across the grass in their childhood backyard. Suddenly, the elder has tears streaming down their cheeks.

When asked if there is anything they want to share with their four-year-old self, the elder responds in the affirmative. "Little one. I am so sorry that I have not acknowledged you, the great effort you have made, for so many years." "You are so amazing to be trying new things, like cartwheels!", "I am so very proud of you!"

The elder requests a chair and remains seated for a time, quietly crying. We as witnesses, stand at their side, remembering to breathe, noticing how their breathing regulates. The elder speaks to the inner child. "I feel so guilty for ignoring you all these years." "For so long I have been trying to get others to notice me when in truth, it was up to me to see you!" "I fear that I have wasted so many years."

The elder, slumped in their chair, begins to sob deeply. "Look at me!", they say to us, the witnesses. "Look at how precious I am!" "Yes!" we share with the elder. "We see you embracing your preciousness." "This young part of you, trying new things!" We acknowledge the courage of the elder to try something new. To mourn the milestone into a new day within themselves. As witnesses, we continue to support. "We hear you say that you feel guilty – is there more you want to say to the four-year-old about feeling guilty?"

The elder, now breathing calmly, tells us that they have nothing more to share. What do we see as the next support for them? We see that potentially missing from the experience is forgiveness of the guilt that they feel, so we check in with them. "We heard you say that you feel guilty for 'ignoring' this part of you." "How might we support you in forgiving yourself?"

The elder sits up straight, placing a hand below their heart, near their diaphragm. "I feel so foolish." "I forgive me for I fear that I wasted so many years of my life looking for attention when it was up to me all along." "I forgive myself for being so self-centered." A light line of tears flows down their face. "I see me right now."

We ask the elder if they feel complete. We ask if their inner child wants anything from them. Are there any agreements made, moving forward? The elder stands and looks again at the four-year-old mark of the Time Circle. "Is there anything you want from me, little one?", "Anything I can do for you?". The elder steps into the inner child space. Surprising themself, they quickly respond "I want you to look in the mirror and see me every day and SMILE!", "Also, I want you to notice the "cartwheels" of others and acknowledge them for trying." "Help them feel seen."

The elder agrees and we as witnesses ensure that the elder is clear on the agreement. Suddenly, the elder swoops their arms down toward their inner child, seemingly lifting them into an embrace while twirling slowly. The elder comes to stillness, sitting down and closes their eyes, still embracing their inner child. We find ourselves taking deep, cleansing breaths as we observe.

As the elder opens their eyes, their heart expands, and they say to us. "Look at all of you!", "I am so grateful to you for being with me.", "Thank you!" It takes great wisdom to overcome the despair of regret and to be in integrity with the Now. Instead of spiraling into regret, this elder sets the example of what it is to embrace the Wisdom available to us.

The North to the East – Grateful Perspective

Traveling from north to east on the Peace on Purpose circle is the perspective of gratitude. Here is where we can look back over the course of our lives, regardless of the number of years lived, and see, or imagine, how all the "mistakes" were actually there to teach us. How we had opportunities to heal and learn through many different scenarios. Though painful or joyful at the time, we can see, from this perspective, how it all comes together to serve us. How it all is coming together to teach us.

This doesn't mean that everyone's story or perspective of their story reads like a stereotypical Disney ending. There are people of all ages, who by many accounts, have survived gut wrenching learning. It isn't fun and by adding my stories, I have no intention of "insulting" those who a consensus would agree, have been through way more than I have. I mean no disrespect to anyone's process.

The thing is, we do not have a barometer for peoples' pain. We can surmise and compare based on the obvious. We think rational people can agree on the assessment of who seems like a whiny victim for example (though we may not really know why) versus who is 'truly' suffering. That's only useful if comparison is essential and we are certain there is not a deeper reason to uncover. Often people compare when comparison need not be a variable.

Ultimately, do we really know that one pain is worse than the other? That one joy is greater than another? Why compare and judge if one person is crying because they didn't get the job they wanted while someone else is sobbing because their parents threw them out on the streets because they are gay.

And the consequences for losing that job? Maybe when they lost their job, and soon their apartment, they would no longer have a place to offer their friend to live whose parents just threw them out of the house. We never really know what's going on inside of someone. We can, however, become more aware of what is going on inside of us.

For us, the purpose of sharing is to hopefully inspire a healing journey in others. Hug the healing journey we have already been on for years. And as we get to the end of our lives, which could come at any time, we hope to be as whole as we can be and as honest with ourselves as possible.

As we look at life consciously, we choose to honor our souls' curriculum and the learning even though there have been times when we wanted to run from it. We want to keep expanding into the best humans we can be. Whether we believe in a God, higher power or in the very least, believe in being the best human possible, I think we can all agree on striving to be the best human possible in terms of intellectual, physiological growth and caring awareness.

Gratitude! As we glance around the Peace on Purpose circle, we may see the parts of us that had once been stopped at 4 centimeters birthing, for example, and then were later born into our hearts because we loved ourselves and were curious enough to return for the aspects that we left behind. We were willing to transform the blame and nonsense to fertilize our healing and feel more gratitude.

Remember the teen in me that stopped at seven centimeters birthing and was willing to wait until she ran out of cigarettes? She is in my heart too because I have learned to love myself enough to allow the birthing process no matter how long it takes. It is never too late. I retrieved her when I went back to my birth, to honor that I was born female in this life or rather to honor that I was born a luminous being, period.

We know the process may involve layers. We go back as many times as needed. I retrieved her another time when I went back to tell her that she and her body are sacred. Still, my life isn't perfect. I continue to strive for honesty, integrity and an open heart with myself and others as appropriate.

Let's come together to realize our potential and share it with each other. Like climbing the rungs of a ladder, someone reaches below to offer a hand to us as we climb up while we offer a hand to those below us. And so on. Simple steps on a torus of gratitude. Remember the 'how' is important too. From where inside of ourselves are we offering that hand? Is it an angry teenager offering a hand down to someone as she blows smoke in their face as could have been the case with me? With gratitude and understanding for the process we show up with the best "whole" us that we have, and we offer a hand. Peace starts with us.

As for me, I continue to push the universe for the All of my life – let me live from the place of my soul's purpose. Not exactly conducive to my grandmother's wish for me: "find a nice little job and marry one of the boys from our family's friends." Sorry grandma! I didn't follow your advice though my life has felt "small" or rather "deep" much of the time. I will see what the Universe has in store for me.

And to Mr. E, beloved family friend who passed away years ago. He was my dad's friend. I loved him very much. How we debated issues and laughed! He told me that I was marrying the wrong man. "He's not right for you." Mr. E, you were right. The truth was that at the time, I also wasn't "right" for me, and the lessons were well on their way. It unfolded the way it did for the highest good of all concerned.

Looking back, I am so grateful that he, as a father figure, saw me and verbalized the reflection even if I couldn't fully receive the wisdom at the time. And maybe if he had not waited until very near my wedding day to tell me that, I would have leaned on him for the courage to make changes. Retrospect! And still that reflection, a gift from Mr. E, did serve my courage 23 years later. I am grateful.

Practicing gratitude is proven to enhance optimism, increase self-esteem, improve social relations and psychological wellbeing. Gratitude is born from a forgiving awareness which is "for giving" to me, to you and to All. As we move through forgiveness, we become grateful for the truth of the journey – all of it! Even the difficult parts.

When the cartwheels cease and the demand for attention subsides, the cartwheeler hears only their truth. What then? There is the choice to heal and forgive as we have witnessed. *It's all* bullshit, my dad would say. My response was to choose what to do with the potential fertilizer. B.S. is fertilizer if I choose to use it that way. There is the choice to accept what we cannot change, courage to change what we still can and the wisdom to know the difference as offered in the Serenity Prayer.

It is all up to us. We can be honest with ourselves. We have the answers inside of us that can be heard from the voice of wisdom when the voice of fear is quiet. We can hear the difference between wisdom and fear. With wise awareness, we proceed through the steps, in sacred timing, embracing gratitude: Reclaiming. Reframing. Reconciling. Realigning.

Gratitude sometimes is inherent at the time of life events, or it may come in retrospect. Gratitude rises when the heart is open and frees it from captivity. With gratitude flowing, the potential for joy increases.

From the vantage point of the north to the east, we look back over all the life stages with compassion, and poignant gratitude. We understand how we came to be who we are right now and what we are offering to make the world, both inner and outer, a place of Light and gratitude. We keep going.

Chapter 5
Why I walk the Peace on Purpose Journey

I have often gone back to younger times of my life to reassess when I noticed patterns of behavior in myself. As I have grown and aged, I have become aware of parts of me that I sort of "left behind" usually because I didn't address some mental or emotional discomfort experienced in the past. Sometimes, acknowledging gratitude is also an essential part of grounding before leveling up to the next stages of life.

Maybe I avoided the parts left behind because I initially was not aware, was too young or stubborn? I realized the missing pieces, like a puzzle, leave out some essential data that I needed to complete the picture of my life.

Whether consciously aware of it or not, all living things strive to reach their potential. My favorite word is "Entelechy" which basically means "the realization of potential." A simple explanatory image of entelechy is a plant growing in the direction of sunlight to reach its fruition. It is the entelechy of an acorn to be an oak tree. Another example may be the person self-medicating with a drug, behavior or food to name a few, because there is some chemical or emotional need in their body that is striving towards the "balance" of potential. Aware or not, we are all doing it to some degree.

It is our responsibility to guide entelechy towards the positive to the best of our ability. And trust me, if reincarnation is true, which I believe, many of us have been walking into the same wall for lifetimes or repeatedly during one life, trying to get to that balance on the other side.

The thing is, on the first attempt, not everyone finds a way to climb over the wall, walk around it, dig a tunnel under it, burst through it, make it vanish or my dramatic favorite, walk through it. Some of us spend years communing with the wall and decide to make it our good friend. Sound familiar?

Believing that my healing would also indirectly benefit my loved ones ignited a passion in me to pierce a veil that I used to fool myself for years. A veil that I allowed to hold me back, especially in my younger life, even though I continued to heal, like peeling layers of an onion through the years. I recall a veil that involved me sitting on a throne of B.S. which is where I go when I refuse to grow and just want to sit in my pity and feel defeated. A place where I judge others or myself harshly because sometimes, I fear that I might be so decrepit, unworthy, and stupid. Where I am mad at younger parts of me with a vehemence that I would never direct at someone else of those ages and understanding. Where I might mistrust that future ninety-year-old in me. Will she have seen me through? Where I harshly judge others and fear the worst. Where the demons have a direct line to incite fear into my hamster wheeling thoughts. You know that place? Though it may feel crippling at times, it lacks sense. It is a place of nonsense!

As I was authoring this book and its many rewrites, I was in the culmination of several challenging years in my life. I had made financial "mistakes" after getting divorced and I continued reviewing the learning opportunities. At times during the years, the future seemed bleak, especially following the days of covid. I found myself moving back to the east coast after a thirty-year stint in Los Angeles.

On the east coast, I started regaining my roots, and my strength. It was time for me to choose to move forward and to stop resisting the next level of growth. I felt ready to expand and further explore my potential despite the occasional efforts to thwart my growth and sense of higher Self. It was time for Giulia's last stand, so to speak, at least for now. Get through it or put my head down and recede until the chance comes around again perhaps in the next life.

Writing this book is a last stand, of sorts, for me. What happens next? I am living each moment now – I have not receded. The rest will become known to me over "time." *It is all B.S.* I hear my dad saying in my mind urging me onward. I realize that there is such wisdom in the thought that everything is illusion or B.S. In fact, the circle of life and its interconnectedness is infused with illusions.

There was a time when I discovered that the malarkey is comprised of times I have been "wronged." All those wrongs become very heavy baggage over time. True, I might have the illusion of being stronger from carrying that baggage around, and I would rather free myself to use that strength to deepen my resilience and set out to purposefully offer "good" out in the world and celebrate being thankful.

Will we seek to transform the illusion, inviting gratitude to rise or will we leave the B.S. to stew for all or portions of life? Nothing like a fabulous throne atop a mountain of bullshit upon which we can sit, be crowned, and marinate in our limiting beliefs and complaints as we monitor our domain. We might need a shovel to dig our way out! We may not even see a need to dig our way out. To fertilize and transform into being crisply alive and grateful or NOT is a pivotal decision. And as we decide to fertilize, we know the Peace on Purpose steps to take to transform the heart of our perception into Being.

Over the years I have circled back and reconciled the times I was mad at my parents, my husband, and people in general, for example. It may seem easier to blame others for our misfortunes, or rather, blame others for our "learning opportunities" but is it really? Yes, there are circumstances where others legally and ethically should take responsibility for what was done. And it is so important that we maintain awareness as to what is being said internally by the "Mind" and "Connection."

In the Introduction there were examples of "the Mind says" versus the response by "Connection". The reality is that often we waste more of our life force attempting to sustain an unnatural flow while fighting the healing process. Replenishing life force is best sustained by natural flow which is the pursuit of personal responsibility, gratitude and forgiveness. We know how to do this!

It took me well into my thirties to understand that I wanted gratitude guiding the remainder of my life. I also learned that when I do what it takes to heal and forgive, the result is positive effect not only to me, but for the All, the macrocosm. Perhaps, a successful life is one in which forgiveness has been at the forefront of decisions and actions?

The soul would perceive a life focused on forgiveness to be a success though as humans we still grapple with the experience of "good" versus "bad" in our perceptions and definitions of "successful". "Good" and "Bad" is a partnering that exists in this dimension if one chooses to dance with it.

Here's what we know. If a child is being molested, beaten, neglected, we will do everything in our power to make it stop. We cannot change the soul's experience for that child, and we will do our part, as humane humans, to convey to that child that they deserve love and protection as we all do. In the process of protecting the child, we will be mindful to be aware of the judgements we have against the perpetrators. Initially, we will spew the outrage we feel for what has been done to an innocent.

Eventually, we will release and forgive the judgements and anger so we can be as centered as possible. Holding on to the baggage of blame and anger is what creates separation. We can protect the child, spew and release the anger and frustration, and return to our humane center so that we are open to being a loving part of All.

Open to connection, to the best of our ability, even if we find ourselves standing on "the other" side of the Bridge of Curiosity. There is so much separation in this world already. No reason to add to it. We keep doing our best.

Learning in life happens. Some lessons can be gut wrenching. Without comparing the lessons, we all have our own perceptions of gut-wrenching moments in our lives. What if, as a soul, I chose to be born the third girl into my family, with its precise predispositions, both genetically and logistically? For this book, this very well may be a topic considered in another book by a different author. I do, however, invite you to consider the supposition that I chose my "situation" so to set up my soul's learning opportunities to be just as they were.

Basically, did I choose my family of this life's origin to "mess" me up exactly as they did? I say yes and thank you so very much for a job well done! A great show! I don't recommend you buy tickets to see the theater production of "Giulia Teresa Cappelli's Learnings in Life", and if we each seek out the marquee that highlights our earthly names? What might we discover?

Opportunities to choose to learn certain lessons so that our souls can advance to higher consciousness, like advancing from grade school to high school to college, are presented over the course of life, sometimes ad nauseam.

We have free will to decide how to respond and are therefore available to walk into a "lesson wall" as many times and possibly for as many lifetimes as we choose. Me? Walk into the same lesson wall, repeatedly? Of course, I personally have never done this. Wall? What wall?

One gratitude scene from "Giulia Teresa Cappelli's Learnings in Life" that would be projected on the screen to highlight thankfulness was my relationship with my paternal grandmother. She lived on the first level of our house in the Bronx and was my anchor in life. My parents worked, and my sisters were older, so being a latchkey, school age Generation X'er, I was lucky that when I got home, grandma was there ready to feed me pasta and large bowls of listening.

I recall being old enough to ask her if my mother would have more children. As in many families, having a "boy" was the prize and note that I was the third daughter in my family. I remember grandma looking at me with that fierce and loving look that would emanate from her brow. She said, "He wasn't meant to be." "YOU were meant to be."

In writing this, I had tears running down my face, one, because I missed her and two, I thank her for fiercely anchoring in me seeds of life and belonging which I had desperately needed. She was always "home" to me. At times, I still return to hug that five, or six-year-old in me who inquired this of grandma and tell little me the same – "YOU, Giulia, are meant to be and I am so thrilled that you ARE".

Standing along the circle, we know that we always have the choice to see experiences through the gratitude of our hearts and/or damnation of our emotions and judgments. If we really want to heal something for the last time, or anchor in a torus of gratitude that will flow forever, lovingly reclaiming aspects of ourselves along the way becomes the way. USM, founded by Drs. Ron & Mary Hulnick, taught me to be the best student of my own Higher Self.

How do we lighten the load as we traverse the Peace on Purpose journey? We point out the hardship, pain, and illusion. We decide what to fertilize and transform into forgiveness and then follow up and see it through to healing, doing the best that we can do. We work the steps to Reclaim, Reframe, Reconcile and Realign our judgements so we lighten the load of what we carry forward within ourselves.

If we carry, for example, anger with us, we continue to experience and express that old anger in a new present moment. Anger that originated in the "past" is leaking in the present moment. To heal, we exercise the four R's, transforming that which no longer serves, as best as we can.

After having consciously gone through the steps regarding a specific time in life, we basically will have cleared a space thereby easing what was likely previously quite a load. As we empty out a space that once gripped us in "separation," we become more open to identifying gratitude and connection. It is important to then refill the open space with fertilized, forward moving life-force, intention and action.

As one of my teachers would say, if you work to empty a space, fill it with the positive things you are invoking! We fill the area with the inner connection of Reclaim, Reframe, Reconcile and Realign. We do this so that as we are sitting in the theater watching the show with our names on the theater marquee, we are confident that no matter how many struggles we witness, each scene will end with Light. We fill each cleared out space with Light.

As I learned at the University of Santa Monica Spiritual Psychology program, "Growth is a process, not an event!" Incremental improvement and maturity happen in sacred timing. Ultimately, we are the coauthors of our story. We unpack and pack our bags and carry them on this journey. How are we doing? What's the status on the price we pay for our essential baggage?

Are we traveling with "carry on" or checked bags? Are we paying extra fees for the weight? Over time and purpose, instead of carrying bags filled with anger and regret, we lighten the load, transforming our essential items to gratitude and Light. We carry on with levity.

In my thirties I started to face the fact that I had been carrying heavy baggage of mental and emotional pain in life, particularly from events in my early adulthood. I began to understand that healing was a responsibility which would positively impact my life, my children and the greater macrocosm. I started the Peace on Purpose journey to return to the time I was in my early twenties when I thought I was in love because I knew what love was. I got engaged to be married because I knew what compatibility was. I had maybe a semblance of a clue.

During the year of my engagement, after a few disagreements, I had a sense that we were not right for each other and addressed the issues the best I could. We had many discussions, some counseling and ultimately, I went back to sleep. I didn't call off the wedding because I loved him and wasn't mature enough to understand the significance of the wisdom that I was attempting to share with myself.

Bottom line: I did not have the self-esteem to stop the wedding plans and therefore didn't get the lesson learned. Where was the kindness I wanted in my life? How unkind was I to myself? In many ways I married a "potential" because what was present in that relationship was not enough to compatibly nurture me.

My husband was a perfectly fine and good man and likely a better companion for NOT me. I think he would agree the reverse is true too.

Subsequently, I spent many years walking into a very painful "lesson wall" of aloneness, trying to "make it" work, almost forcing myself to bend towards darkness instead of light because I lived up against the shadow of the wall.

I was committed to making it work because I am a very loyal person, and I loved my family. You get the picture? And though on the surface I had a very fine life, what I was feeling inside, when I allowed myself to notice, was something very different.

Now imagine that I stick with it, which I did. Raise a family, grow myself as best as I can as a woman but as a wife, I settle for crumbs of love. Note that I didn't say that he offered crumbs – my perception was that of choosing mostly from an array of crumbs because years prior, by accepting the relationship even though it was not enough to compatibly nurture me, I had already made the unconscious choice to deny myself the feast I craved. As a mother, I settled for not being the happiest and best mother I could have been. Retrospect is just that.

I was living an illusion and convinced myself that the "lesson wall" was in a perfect location and no remodeling was needed. I was stuck. Back to imagining it is happening in the present, let's say it's my 10th, 20th, 23rd wedding anniversary, let me hang *this* wedding picture on *this* wall.

Every time I walk by *that* photo and look at myself, what type of thoughts and emotions might you imagine are evoked? If people could hear me talk in my head, what did I say? Come on, let's get some educated guesses going: "You, stupid idiot", "Why did you do this to yourself?" I can be so mean to me! Sometimes I just gave the stink eye to myself as I walked by.

Of course, my self-talk lashed out at my husband too. How rich might many of us be as contestants on the 'Blame Game' or 'Can You Top

This?' comparing burdens? "You are the winner!" "You are righteous and have been wronged by life more than the other contestants!" "Congratulations!" Yes! Add my crown and scepter to the vision as I sit on my throne of righteousness and blame, receiving game prizes. What prizes do we receive for being righteous? I wanted to find neutral ground. I recall the Rumi poem: *Out beyond ideas of wrongdoing and rightdoing, is a field. I'll meet you there.* I went looking for the field.

When I dared to notice, I realized that I was hurting. Who to blame? In the beginning and the end, I am responsible for me, including the filters I used through which to see my husband, myself and others.

There were moments when I dared to have compassion for that beautiful young woman, and lovely looking couple, so full of good intentions. Good intentions are just that: "good" and not necessarily ever enough.

Here's the thing. At that time in my thirties when I was deeply looking back at my life, if I were to put the puzzle pieces of my life together there would not be any missing pieces. It would have resembled a complete puzzle, but if I looked more closely, which I dared to do, I noticed that amongst the, let's say, Monet expressed images are a few by Picasso. What the heck? How did I miss that?

Luckily, I finally listened to my wisdom. I found the incongruence because there was a deafening crescendo of awareness that fought to get my attention. Picture an old Italian woman dressed in black hitting me over the head repeatedly with a loaf of bread. But I almost missed it because "Illusions rock sweet snoring souls" a line from a poem I wrote in 1999. Who knows how many more years I would have spent snoring, dreaming of a complete set of my life images exhibited as Monet puzzle pieces.

The Picasso image of my face on a Monet body drove me to evaluate *that wall* as I paced like a caged animal. The moment of personal responsibility hit me when I realized that I had good intentions and then I allowed myself to be hurt. I was in a cage, and I had the key to get out all along. Easy to say and hard to imagine that I let it go for so long. I wanted my marriage to be successful.

Of course, life decisions are rarely that simple when raising children and self, loving one's family, maintaining financial issues, and eventually feeling generalized anxiety etc. If I had to do it all again? Well, as a woman, I would not have gotten married and instead would have spent more time courting myself, knowing and loving myself, completing my graduate school education and certifications and growing up professionally, emotionally and mentally. As a mother? I would do it all again, to have my children be exactly who they are. Questions for retrospect are unfair to matters of the heart.

I believe I would have become acquainted with some form of "lesson wall" even if I had delayed marriage. There is no avoiding being faced with the learning opportunity listed on my soul's curriculum. Choose to move through it, not move through it and/or visit all the variations in between. Regardless, lessons will be presented until one "passes", or rather, moves through, each "test". It's a conscious or unconscious choice to face it or ignore it. Facing it will involve the option to move through the Peace on Purpose journey or using another viable method that resonates for us.

But what about those Picasso pieces challenging the congruency of my Monet? Can you feel my impatience? Let's face it, by 44 years old, I wanted Monet dang it! I was a strong woman. For many years I lived against my natural flow and managed to do a fine job. No one asked me to do that!

If I can do that as well as I did, what might my life be when I AM living in flow with the natural direction of my pulsating Entelechy? I wanted to find out! So, with conscious intention in the fall of 2010 I started the process and I announced to the Universe that I wanted to be shown the truth of my life and to live from *that* place. I began to push myself mentally, emotionally, physically and to further nurture myself spiritually.

I pointedly set intentions and then I put my intentions into action, assessing the alignment of the choices I made. Intentions, without taking action in support thereof, are mere thoughts. Once I ask the Universe for assistance, and take action to meet the Universe halfway, then the Universe responds.

To put the intention of being shown the truth of my life into action, I started hiking hills to activate my legs and my body. I physically, mentally and emotionally revived the Way of the Sacred Directions which was my graduate school theory of counseling paper. I went to therapy to see what else I could uncover. I invited my husband to join me for a meeting with an attorney to start the conversation when counseling felt more like being on a talk show than I felt it was helping us. I played my flutes to feel my spirit. My breath of life.

Were the actions I was taking in alignment with my natural flow? What about the flow of my marriage and family? Let's pause for a moment. I am not advocating for selfishness. I believe it is very important to see the impact my choices have on others, especially loved ones. From microcosm to macrocosm and vice versa, remember? At some point, when one begins to feel like part of that wall is looming over them and help is not manifesting from the places and people one has requested assistance, it may be time for a change in direction. It was time for me.

Honestly, if I had not adjusted at that point, I would have contracted a disease due to the prolonged lack of ease I was living in my marriage.

On the surface, my life looked easy. How I comport myself as I initiate the change in direction determines the value of the outcome. Selfishness? No. Self-loving? Yes, and definitely, in critical timing, and in alignment with my natural flow despite how incredibly painful it was and is in moments that surprise me still.

Let's pick up those Picasso pieces and replace them with the Monet softness, light and beauty to complete the image of my life in that moment. No offense to Picasso, the work of art was Monet, and congruency was the goal. I circle back because I refuse to look at a Picasso face of me depicted on the Monet of my soul. I stand at the section of the circle that represented my chronological age when I noticed the mental and emotional distress. I acknowledge myself for the choices I made and for doing the best that I could at the time.

Now I know better, so I am doing better and to do the best I can, it is imperative that I reclaim those younger parts of me that I had rejected: To the me who decided to get married, "You, stupid idiot!", "Why did you do this to yourself?" Start the process to Reclaim, Reframe, Reconcile and Realign.

This is not intended to be one stop shopping nor is it intended to consume our time and lives. This process is meant to be willingly worked at least several times at a deep level so that we create an inner pathway for walking the Time Circle, so it becomes natural to do so.

Ultimately, we hope to be able to approach most life events with inner healing by taking responsibility and cleaning up the "mess" as we are making it, thereby replenishing with gratitude. We can do this if we have awareness and muscle memory for the healing path of forgiveness.

This is an average path. There are ranges of pain and dysfunction that have debilitated some people and may cause the option of starting this process to take longer. We may never be willing to consciously heal. It may take a lifetime to be ready to choose responsibility for our own healing especially when we have been traumatized as an innocent. Hence the reason it is suggested that the path initially be witnessed by an invested friend, coach or therapist and the reason we bow to sacred timing.

"You stupid idiot!", "Why did you do this to yourself?" When I was in my thirties and forties, in peeling layers of healing for myself, I faced the young woman in me who decided to get married in her early twenties. I stood at the west of the circle, the onset of Adulthood. The place where we begin to Harvest the blessings of the truth of who we are and faced myself.

I began to state the truth to the twenty-something year old in me. "Whatever your good intentions were back then, they were motivated by love despite some of the painful outcomes." "I am so pissed at the years I lost when I could have been better and grown into so much more." "I acknowledge your persevering despite the pain." I know you want to use the shovel for what sounds like B.S. Me too. I had to start somewhere! Just a little more patience.

"Now I heed my wisdom more easily and I listen to my bones." "Even though I thought I was an idiot for the choices I made, I know deep down that I was not stupid." Sounds like a lot of mental stroking, right? Look at me being nice to myself! Fake it until we make it. That's the warm-up because as I say the upcoming self-forgiveness statements, in the way I learned at USM, there were a few gobs of snot emitted as I cried. Be grateful there are no pictures.

Not every exchange has to be dramatically emotional. I will add, however, if there is no snot or equivalent poignancy felt, and you are working on a very deep issue, you might want to keep searching for just the right words that grab at your heart and then release it into expansion. I cannot stress enough the critical importance of finding the specific words that take hold of your heart and release it into expansion complete with poignancy or sobs. Hold. Release. Expand.

After the superficial statements, I begin to find the energy stream that speaks for my heart. As I speak from my heart, I am in effect *Reclaiming* that twenty-something aspect of me. "I forgive myself for judging myself as a stressed mother who could have been happier because my kids deserved the best of me. Especially my first two kids who had me when I was less aware." "I let my kids down because I should have been better." "I let myself down because I could have been so much more joyful." "I let myself down because I could have accomplished so much more with my personal and professional life." "I forgive myself for judging myself as letting my marital stress disrupt my children." "They didn't deserve that." "I forgive myself for judging myself as stupid and wasting myself."

I keep going, searching for the words that grab deeply at my heart, knocking the wind out of me. "As failing to provide for myself." "As having given me away." "As having sacrificed my light to the shadow of that wall." "No one asked me to do that." This is the point that makes me cry deeply, choking for air: "As having sacrificed my light to the shadow of that wall." "No one asked me to do that." "I did that to myself."

I state it several times until I can breathe through reciting the words. Sometimes even after a few rounds and gobs of snot I hear the judgment rise again: "Well, maybe I was stupid!" and I go back into self-forgiveness until I no longer hear myself judging me so harshly but rather, I simply assess and state what was and what is. *Reconcile.* "As having sacrificed my light to the shadow of that wall." (*Hold*). "No one asked me to do that." (*Release*). "I did that to myself." (*Expand*) into aligning with the truth.

It really can be a process like peeling layers of an onion. *Reframe* "The truth is I am a wise, strong and so loving of a being." "The truth is I am finding my way." "The truth is I am not a failure." "I am a work of art in progress." "I am a Mistress piece." Why should I be a masterpiece? Geez. These gender words! "The truth is, we grew a beautiful family together that is cherished and precious." "We are so blessed to have each other." My family is where I feel gratitude. I love my children fiercely and honor the memories of "home." I realize that coming home to myself is an essential illuminated path for my personal growth.

Now I know I can call for inner reinforcements and walk through the wall should I ever find myself again surrounded by a similar architecture resultant of my unconscious, albeit well-intentioned choices. I move forward in my life, *Realigned.* The wall has been remodeled. I imagine myself walking through it.

If I don't retrieve lost parts of me and express gratitude for some aspects of the process, how do I expect to reach the end of my life, which could come at any time, as whole and complete as possible? It is my goal to live and die as whole and as grateful as I can possibly be thereby doing my part in taking responsibility for my healing and allowing that energy to raise the vibration for the macrocosm as well. I do not want to be an old woman who thinks only about herself. I want to be giving back to the younger generations, and learning from them, if they will have me.

Why do I consciously partake of this Peace on Purpose journey? With the tools available to reclaim experiences from the past, I reconcile and reframe in the truth and forgiveness of what I know in the Now, with flowing Gratitude as I strive to realign and to "do better" or "be better". As Maya Angelou once stated to Oprah Winfrey "When you know better, you do better". The Peace on Purpose journey invites the forgiveness of "knowing better" so that I may be gratefully present and "do better" for myself, others and the world with forward momentum and inner stillness.

I circle my story because ongoing, I want to be as honest and transformative with myself as I can be. Because I strive for wholeness, I progress towards completion instead of repeating patterns of unfinished learning opportunities. I walk the Peace on Purpose circle because I refuse to enter another life phase where I step willingly into a locked cage as I tuck the key into my pocket. Because I know what I want. I want the complete Monet of my Soul.

Onward.

Chapter 6
Gratitude Reality Stories

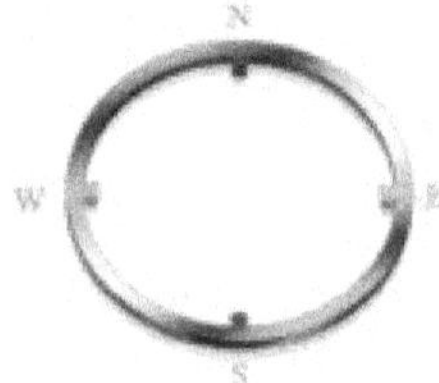

Gratitude lives between the lines of our individual and collective stories. It is not a trophy of good fortune but rather an essential metronome of the heart's Lub Dub. By cultivating gratitude, we ensure strength of heart for the human experience.

The purpose of the Gratitude Reality Stories is to illuminate some basic scenarios that may occur in life. Perhaps we have personally experienced something akin to some of these stories or we know someone who has. By reading their stories we glean wisdom and allow it to anchor in our hearts.

There are many scenarios and stories of people not depicted here. Please note that energetically all the stories leading to grateful insight are welcomed. We are encouraged to read the below with an open heart and mind knowing which other tales we would add to this group to make it more complete.

<u>*JADE'S CIRCLE STORY*</u>

Jade tried for seven years to forgive her husband after he admitted to having cheated. Her husband tried to earn back her love and trust. He basically bowed to almost her every wish hoping that she would trust him again and they could rebuild their love and family.

Life went on and Jade was obsessed with the broken vow. She had anxiety, now worsened since the cheating, and feared other people would hear about the betrayal. She was embarrassed.

She had done nothing wrong, why should she be a gossip topic when it was her husband's mistakes? How dare he!

Jade grew up being adored by her family. It was as if she was meant to be adored. She 'should' be taken care of forever. She had done nothing wrong. In fact, she married young and is still learning to lead herself. Maybe she followed him for too long or perhaps she just allowed him to direct and lead her. In the early years, she had often looked to him to make decisions or to give instruction. Was that being adored and taken care of? Had she ever adored herself? She wonders if not having forgiven him was in fact a rebellion for the years she allowed his control of her.

What do we notice about Jade? She feels she is completely innocent and therefore is *always* deserving of reward. The thing is, Jade has made a choice to keep her heart closed. She refuses to face her anxiety that existed long before the cheating. She is beginning to see that she is a variable in the equation of her marriage. In the very least, she is a variable in the equation of her life.

She makes room for different perspectives by acknowledging that beyond dealing with infidelity, perhaps she let herself be led and then controlled and is defiant about forgiveness. People do forgive each other and enter back into a loving relationship with deeper appreciation and better tools for a happy and viable union. Maybe for her, forgiving would lead her back to a perception of living under a thumb.

For some people there is only the black or white version of their story. For Jade, there may never be a balanced Ying Yang approach to her perspective of self in this life. For this portion of the Peace on Purpose journey, Jade has reached an impasse, and her family breaks apart with divorce. She will move on, possibly learning to lead herself, with the very heavy baggage of unforgiven judgements.

Someday she might choose to do the work to support healing and forgiveness; lighten the baggage load and open her heart to herself and embrace the self-loving leader within. If not, she will likely spin her hamster wheeling story of how she was wronged, and she will find a different man to carry the bags for her. He will adore her, and she will look up to him. The universe will decide the next lesson plan in the curriculum from which Jade will make her choices. For now, she gratefully summons the strength to move forward, hopefully discovering a process to release anger and pain.

RAY'S CIRCLE STORY

Ray was five years-old and living in pain. Home life was a complete mess and to call it a home was a joke. He attended kindergarten at the local public school followed by going to clinic to work with a group of kids and a therapist. At the age of five, Ray was already sick of life.

After an outburst at clinic, Ray ran out of the group therapy room, down the hall towards the exit and slumped down onto the floor. Still angrily grasping the paper upon which he was to draw a picture of the people who lived at home, Ray began to crumple the blank paper. Breathing heavily, he sat, looking at the floor between his feet. The counselor walked briskly to catch up to him and slumped down next to him just in time to hear Ray state that "Life is shit and I want to die."

The therapist took a deep breath and offered Ray her piece of paper in case he wanted to crumple another. Ray obliged, grunted and both ripped and bunched it up simultaneously. Tears running down his cheeks, he turned his body towards his papers. He was open to anyone in the hallway. He did not turn to hide his tears or skew his body position. He leaned forward and began to uncrumple a piece of paper and breathe deeply.

Joining him, the counselor took the other bunched up paper and began to smooth it out, opening it while breathing audibly. Together, they did this a few times.

The wisdom of Ray, perhaps communing with a wiser part of himself was displaying an analogy for life: a clean pressed piece of paper, crumpled with the force of the death of innocence and flattened with cleansing breaths revealed the lines of strife and resilience of life.

This particular five-year-old who stated that "Life is shit" and "I want to die" was actively engaging an aspect of self, who, witnessed by the counselor, was throwing him a lifeline. *"Remember to breathe"* the *counselor stated as they sat together, crumpling and flattening their papers while breathing, intermittently through his tears.*

After a few minutes, Ray leaned on the counselor, resting his head near to her shoulder. Turning his face into her armpit, one arm reached out across her body for a hug, that was more like a "hang" as his body, exhausted with emotions, clung to her. The counselor hugged him in return, allowing herself to be crumpled and flattened with each breath that they took, crumpling and opening, crumpling and opening.

With each breath and opening, the counselor imagined planting seeds of love for Ray. Like lines on the paper, the scars might always be there and yet, the pictures can still be drawn, and someday the "shit" can always be fertilizer for something positive. Seeds of love.

TROY'S CIRCLE STORY

Troy opened his eyes, feeling his cheek on the floor in a pool of saliva and grit. The first thing he saw was sunlight creeping in through a gap in the paint on a window that was painted black. He was in a crack house somewhere in the city, fixated on that tiny stream of light. He had no idea how he got there or the level of danger he was in at that moment.

Slowly, he collected himself, his hands vaguely touched himself all over as if to take inventory of what remained of him. Troy was grateful to be alive. In fact, he doesn't even know how he survived. He had awakened in odd places before with little memory but this time it was different.

Troy felt like he was almost in complete darkness. He had nearly no light left in him to use to fool himself into thinking that he could rally for the next "celebration". He tasted the grimy floor from the back of his teeth, Troy's hands investigated his face and head and surmised that he had an open wound on his skull and dried blood running down the back of his head.

There was a time when Troy had a bright future. He worked hard and partied harder through college and grad school. He was handsome, had a great family and friend base. He had women who wanted him all the time. He had it all?

Somewhere, though, he was still looking for himself. The nervous energy he had as a kid, the anxiety, was not fostered well in the school system. He was a busy kid. He felt pressure as the oldest to be the best as an example for the other family members. Somewhere along the way all that anxiety got quashed to a simmer of alcohol and recreational drugs which continued for many years. Troy was living in shadows. His friends had no idea that after they all went home at night, Troy instead went to other bars.

That particular day, Troy didn't believe his own lies. He woke up in shadow reaching for a tiny stream of light seeping in through the painted windowpane. That day, he was grateful to be alive. There was gratitude for tiny streams of light that provided direction. That day became the day he acknowledged that he never again wanted to taste dirt and grime and he got help. After all, peace starts with him.

After rehabilitation, Troy became committed to the AA process serving himself and others through over 30 years sobriety. Through countless discussions with his sponsor, over time, Troy realigned with the anxious younger self who knows now that Troy believes in him. Currently, Troy has gratitude and a heart of service that benefits others. He knows well that growth is a process to be cared for and honored, in the moment. Troy does better as he knows better and is grateful to be alive and in service to life.

ANYA'S CIRCLE STORY

Anya is thirty years old. Their childhood is a blur of time spent in a dysfunctional and violent home, foster care and mental hospitals. Anya is just beginning to imagine how it may feel to "relax". To exhale and mean it. It has taken them years of therapy and hugging trees to get to where they are today.

Today Anya is choosing a career path and applying to college at the age of thirty. In their childhood years, they were severely abused and neglected; they spent countless hours locked in a dog crate from the ages of two to four years old. With the assistance of some amazing clinicians, the ones who care beyond the parameters of the limited Medicaid systems, Anya has been reclaiming fragmented aspects of their "story" and re-scripting narrative so to acknowledge the real truth about themself.

How devastating to be a luminous being locked in a cage, uncared for! Anya loves to be out in nature, especially to be near trees. They remind them that they can be stable and flexible while providing their own oxygen and potentially bear fruit. When in the crate, as a little one, Anya imagined a tree growing up in the corner of the bars, where the bars converged and the wiring got a little thicker, like a tree trunk. The tree became a safe haven in their mind when they needed to escape reality.

Anya is exploring life from the perspective of being inherently safe and worthy of safety. How could these people have done this to them? It is very painful to grow beyond blaming them. Yes, they will always be responsible both legally and morally for what they did. And now, after all Anya has been through, as an adult themself, Anya is mustering the strength to go back into the past to keep retrieving pieces of them that belong to them. Pieces of self that belong only in Anya's trusted heart. Anya is actively re-scripting portions of their life, to reveal the truth to themself. The truth of their worthiness.

Anya is getting to know self. What do they like? What interests them? Anya is slowly harvesting the self and making decisions that align. Perhaps they might be a teacher but are not sure yet. They did, however, start volunteering for an organization that plants trees in urban areas. Anya is grateful for trees.

After many trips to the past around the Time Circle, Anya dares to walk the Peace on Purpose circle forward to speak to themself when they are sixty years old. This is a courageous path for Anya to take because they feel so very unsteady about who they are right now.

Anya steps along the west of the circle, further towards the north. They stop at the place they imagine they will stand at age sixty and turn, looking to the west towards their thirty-year-old position. Anya takes a deep breath, glances at their coach and then closes their eyes. Sixty-year-old Anya adjusts their weight and gets very grounded in the way they are standing; feet hip width apart fully facing the younger self. Anya opens their eyes and stares toward the ground at the thirty-year mark. Anya's breathing quickens and they begin to cry. They open their mouth to speak and pause, finding the right words:

"Courageous Anya", the sixty-year-old self begins as tears roll down their cheeks. "I cannot even begin to thank you for your heart and your strength." "Because of you, I am standing here, strong, healthy and with heart." "I love you". "You are a life warrior!" Wiping their tears, sixty-year-old Anya clasps their hands together in a prayer gesture and becomes silent. Anya's coach stands quietly, breathing deeply.

Anya then walks back to the thirty-year-old position and faces the thirty-year-old self. Anya takes a breath and begins to tremble. Falling to their knees and sobbing, Anya speaks to the older self "I cannot even imagine that I am still alive and so strong!" "Just feeling you makes me hopeful for the future."

As Anya looks towards where their sixty-year-old self was standing they visualize one of the trees they recently planted having grown another thirty years, well rooted and present to look over the big picture of the future. Anya slightly exhales and smiles briefly. "I know that I will make good enough choices and no matter what, I have the strength to do good enough."

They take time to breathe, exhale and pause. Looking at their coach, Anya shares "I cannot fully explain the emotion running through my body." "I know that I feel different". "Like I need to stretch and bend my body into new positions." Anya stretches their body, reaching their arms down to their feet and then up to the sky. Taking a deep breath, they wave their outstretched arms back and forth as they exhale. Essentially, Anya plants the tree of Self.

Anya is still learning to trust that they will show up for self and to find a way to meet their own needs. Sacred timing.

<u>KELSEY'S CIRCLE STORY</u>

Kelsey had been walking the Time Circle for many years. Sometimes with friends and witnesses, sometimes on their own. They loved striving for more compassion for self and other; for more understanding and expansion after releasing pain and blame. They even reached out to future selves and formed bonds with parts of them yet to be.

What they had not counted on was missing something. They often guided themself alone around the Time Circle though they were frequently available to stand and witness others. They walked alone and therefore usually healed alone, rarely sharing the experiences with someone else unless it came up in conversation.

Kelsey found themself facing their own wisdom. When conjuring up images of healing to offer as suggestions for a friend to paint for a project, they recalled a time at the end of a retreat weekend, following an explosive awakening, a time when as a participant, they had been offered a chance to be "held" and "nurtured" and instead, skipped that part of the retreat session, ending their evening and readying for bed.

Standing at the west of the Time Circle and asking themself why years ago they skipped out on that portion of the retreat session, they realized that they had denied themself beautiful healing after such an expansive and explosive processing of emotions. Gratefully, this time, they had a friend present to stand as witness to the Time Circle journey. Kelsey walked to the 29-year-old mark, their age at the time of the retreat, sat on the ground and outstretched their arms to receive and hold their inner 29-year-old self.

They sat, Kelsey holding and nurturing their younger self allowing to be received what had been rejected years prior. After a time, and several deep breaths and several drops of tears, blown dry in the wind, Kelsey opened their eyes and looked directly at their witness. The witness, wanting to be sure they understood correctly, walked slowly around the circle and stood next to Kelsey and took a breath. Kelsey, finding it hard to speak, and not wanting to get caught up in their head, again, looked directly at the witness conveying a desire with their eyes while nodding once indicating permission.

The witness then sat on the ground, behind Kelsey and outstretched their arms. Kelsey leaned back and offered themself to the nurturing embrace and began to cry years of "holding" they had done alone. Years of being strong so not to make waves at home when they were very young, so they could feel safe. Years of "holding" self in check so to be available to others. Years of holding back their own fears about the strength of their vulnerability because suddenly the realization pulsed through their body; their open vulnerability was not only a strength for themself; it was also a gift to others.

Visualizing the healing image for the painting, Kelsey imagined their grandmother sitting on the ground behind their friend holding them, as the witness, holding Kelsey, leaned back into the grandmother's embrace. Behind Kelsey's grandmother was their father. Behind their father, their great aunt appeared. Behind their great aunt emerged what looked to be a luminous being, glowing with compassion and goodwill.

Kelsey took a breath and lovingly held their inner 29-year-old. In the lap of the inner 29-year-old, cradled, Kelsey realized sat their inner six-year-old. In the lap of the six-year-old sat another luminous being holding Kelsey as an infant. Everyone sitting along the line of nurturing leaned into the embrace and began to breathe in a regulated beat to the rhythm of love, gratitude and compassion. A pulsating Lub Dub embrace.

Kelsey imagined an audience of onlookers. They could almost hear the supportive sounds of their Ancestors and Guides breathing in concert.

SAM'S CIRCLE STORY

Troy's friend Sam drank a lot growing up. Alcohol and drugs were already a regular part of the evening long before life got so complicated. Troy knew that Sam was having trouble keeping his job. Sam had a few kids, and his wife had very expensive taste and plans. She had just lost her job. Sam was struggling to keep up with demand. Part of him was disappearing into alcohol.

Troy had been too messed up to intervene though he tried to stay in touch. Sam loved his family and struggled to feel real connection and partnership with himself and with his wife. If Troy had seen Sam's financial accounts, he would have been more concerned. Sam was careening into a financial disaster. He was too ashamed to ask anyone else for help. He felt he had failed his family and that they would be better off without him.

One afternoon some part of Sam just snapped and turned to stone. He could no longer handle the inner strife he experienced in each moment. He felt completely hopeless and embarrassed.

Sam took his own life. At one point, he was grateful for the love he felt for the family he failed and for the hope to be at peace. He hoped his family would understand.

Let's take a moment to send love, light and prayers to everyone who has encountered this pain.

Sam was grateful for the choice. Sadly, that is no consolation for all the loved ones left behind wondering what they could have done differently to elicit communication with Sam that would have provided a different ending. Though we may all have our opinions, we are not here to judge the curriculum of anyone's soul, nor the choices people make interacting with their lessons. Spirit has a different perspective.

We do see that Sam's story injects curriculum into the soul journeys of his loved ones. These are people who on a good day might prefer to have ice water thrown on their faces to rouse them from the pain in their hearts. These are also people who learn something different in life because of tragedy. These are people who deserve the last piece of pie.

Instead of accepting it, they will lovingly prepare and bake a pie and set it to cool near the window, and never eat it.

It becomes an offering to life. A way to release a little bit of the helplessness they feel until one day, when they are ready, the "forgiveness" pie is donated at healing gatherings; Troy takes the pies to an AA potluck. They get sent to Al-Anon, grief groups and sometimes even to waiting rooms of very expensive recreational life choices that Sam couldn't afford but wished he could offer to his family.

The bakers, in this case, the people left behind, rarely ever know who got the pie they offered to others. Forgiveness metaphors are love in action and operate under the laws of sacred timing. At the very least we can all be grateful for being inspired by the people who support each other to carry on, no matter what.

JO'S CIRCLE STORY

Jo had a fairly typical childhood without many issues. Jo didn't always feel that included in groups as a child and managed to have some close friends who were in the same boat. Jo and their friends all floated through middle and high school managing life's malarkey as a group. Mom and Dad were there. Even when their parents divorced and Jo got another dad, though there was upheaval, they got through it. Jo felt loved.

After high school Jo got a partial scholarship to university and eventually got a decently paying job. Jo found a partner. They had a bunch of pets and didn't want kids. They enjoyed traveling and sharing life with friends and family. Jo lives life from a place of gratitude and shares in celebrations with loved ones.

Jo's path is an example of one without too many bumps and bruises. Jo could have chosen to blame others for the pain and suffering experienced and yet managed to get through to adulthood without much baggage.

Jo is curious. They ask questions and communicate well with others. If there is strife, Jo tends to stay away and instead invest in people who better reflect their values and behaviors. When Jo circles back, Jo finds there was some fear around the time of their parents' divorce. Jo recalls memories of their father's neighbor, at the new house.

The Chins were like an embrace for Jo when they were staying with dad who provided a comforting distraction from the weirdness of settling into a weekend life with one parent in a new abode. A second marriage with a combined family of four kids, there was always food and banter available. The activities assisted Jo in easing into a life changing event. Jo is ever thankful for the generosity of the Chin family. Their loving example prepared Jo for their future stepfather and stepbrother.

Jo is a fine example of someone living with a grateful heart – the kind of person others might dislike just because they seem pretty happy with an easy-going life and few complaints. We just don't all have the same soul curriculum! Nor are we meant to live duplicate lives. I am not sure what to tell you. If we are a bit envious of Jo, we might take a walk around the Time Circle to discover the origins of that envy.

<u>JESS' CIRCLE STORY</u>

Jess's older brother died in a car crash on his way to fetch her from a party. Jess was supposed to have gone home with a friend but missed the ride. Jess has since folded in upon herself. She felt guilty and struggled with severe depression.

Jess's parents, also stricken with grief, found themselves at a greater loss in not being able to reach Jess's heart as they barely had healed their own. Jess refused to circle her story and refused continued therapy. Jess already had one suicide attempt because she did not want to live in a world without her brother. Jess refused to entertain the word "peace."

"Jess", "Are you willing to take a walk and talk about what's been happening?"

Jess looks at the floor, "No" she states, holding her breath.

"Jess." "How are you doing in school this semester?"

Jess looks at the window. "No."

"Jess." "I am going to keep checking in with you to make sure you are safe and that you know I care." "I am not giving up on you." "I trust you are taking the time you need."

Jess glances in the direction of their voice. "Okay."

Sacred timing. Jess is grateful for time alone and for knowing someone is there.

"Jess, would you like something to eat?"

Jess responds that she does not. Once the person has left the area, Jess goes and fixes herself something to eat and returns to her room where she sits on her bed not noticing how her body is holding on to tension.

The day may come when Jess is willing to receive from a caring person in her life. Perhaps she will circle back one day and forgive herself for having missed the ride home that caused her brother to be out driving that fateful night. With loving assistance and willingness, she will consider how to surrender.

The truth is, she missed her ride home just being a teenager, imperfect like anyone else. She did not plan to inconvenience anyone and never wanted harm to come. With each breath and mass of streaming tears, she considers releasing guilt to forgiveness. One day when asked if she is willing to discuss how she feels about losing her brother she will accept the offer and begin that part of the journey. One day her rib cage will fully expand and relax as she takes deep cleansing breaths.

Sacred timing.

LENNY'S CIRCLE STORY

Lenny spent a lot of time out with friends. Often, they went out for dinner or played video games. His close friends were well acquainted with stories about how Lenny's father was a cheater and alcoholic and barely spent time with Lenny or his sisters when they were growing up.

Any time conversation turned toward holidays or families, Lenny would start telling tales about his dad. His friends, though they loved him, would cringe a bit because once again, they were uncomfortable feeling Lenny's intense pain. They have heard Lenny share his pain, telling the stories with such intensity as if it was all still happening in the present. When Lenny would get on a roll, his friends were beginning to change the subject or leave the room. One close buddy challenged Lenny during a family story when Lenny claimed to have healed his childhood pain. "Then why are you still talking about it?" "It feels to me like you are still a little kid quivering with rage and hurt."

Lenny's story is common because Lenny does feel like he healed the pain of childhood associated with his past. The thing is, it is likely that Lenny the little kid (inner child Lenny) is still upset and tells the story every chance he gets! Little Lenny is trying to sort through it all and wants comfort because he was wronged and didn't deserve it. When adults heal through their intellect and don't know how to peel more layers that include their inner child, intellectually they have sorted through the past situation. The emotions of the chronological younger part of them may still be hurting.

Lenny realizes that his good friend, the one who challenged him, is right. He does have a pattern of telling the same story. He reaches out to another friend who refers him to her therapist and sends him the Find Peace on Purpose book for inspiration. At his friend's behest, Lenny pulls out photo albums from his childhood.

As he looks though the pictures, he notes all the different thoughts and emotions running through his being. There is one photo that catches his attention. He sits up, adjusts his pillow, and sinks back into the couch as he turns the page entitled "Summer 1980 Vacation" with a family picture under the caption. He feels his intestines cramp and discovers that he could smile at some memories while tearing up at others.

If we were looking in through the living room window of Lenny's house and had magical lenses, we might see Lenny sitting with his arm around a boy, little Lenny, as they both reviewed the memory album. Lenny would dry the eyes of the little boy, as he hugs him tightly and kisses him on top of his head. Just before we turn to leave, we would see the little boy looking up at Lenny as Lenny turns his head to gaze at the boy. Their eyes locked on each other, as ours are locked on them, we would all take a deep breath. Precious. When one person heals, the witnesses benefit too. Eventually, Lenny's stories will be shared, and they will inspire others to heal, and look deeper for peace on purpose.

KYRIE'S CIRCLE STORY

Kyrie was born surrounded by hope. They were a luminous baby; joyful, easy-going, curious. Blessed with a big dose of physical intelligence in their five years of life, they were growing into a warrior! There were a lot of irrational and control issues in Kyrie's family which was very scary to a developing young person who was trying to make sense of love and safety in the messaging received. Regardless of the confusion and illusions of a happy family, the light of Kyrie's spirit, so connected to life, loved ones and nature, did its best to make sense of the conflicting experiences they survived.

Too young to cognitively "know" what they were facing day to day, they persevered by creating a pathway, one on which it was certain that their sense of self was true. By the age of five, with Halloween approaching, Kyrie could be seen in a holiday store staring from a distance at the very scary mannequin witches and goblins for sale. Something inside of Kyrie urged them forward to face their fear.

Kyrie was determined to know the true nature of the decorations. In the process, Kyrie revealed their own true nature. Dropping the babysitter's hand, Kyrie requested that the sitter follow and "stay next to me," they instructed. Kyrie walked up to every frightening boisterous and animated human size decoration.

With the light of courage, and support nearby, Kyrie reached out a finger and poked each and every one, directly facing their fears. Kyrie's true nature is that of a light warrior. They illuminated the truth, turning the scary into the "just make believe" items as they had determined.

Kyrie's story is a gift on a few levels because not only does this child set an example to all adults about learning to face one's fears in sacred timing, additionally, their story reminds us that the Time Circle does not discriminate. Kyrie, to the very best of their ability, has already been harvesting self like an adult; taking responsibility to face their Halloween demons and like a wise elder, confronted their fears because they saw through to the truth.

Kyrie, as an elder, was giving back to the younger generation which in this case was self and ironically the sitter who was chronologically much older! Kyrie also requested the support of a witness to walk with them which we know to be an important aspect of the journey. It takes wisdom to ask for assistance. Kyrie is grateful for the ability to pierce the veil of illusion.

They are too young to comprehend, but some day they will know that they learned long ago to walk the illuminated path of courage. Kyrie, a wise elder at the age of five, is an example to us all. Over time and depending on their "how to be" as they continue to grow up, illusions will bow to their warrior presence as the dark and scary corners near them flood with light.

When Kyrie becomes a teenager, with understanding, they will begin the first of many Time Circle journeys and will do their best to Reconcile and Reframe the dark; and Realign and Reclaim the light of hope that was always their birthright.

FRANKIE'S CIRCLE STORY

Frankie always had a zest for life! Now 87 years young he continues to see life from the optimist's perspective because Frankie owns his stuff and takes responsibility for self. He had the courage in life to be wrong so as he knew better, he did better. He is living a good life! He has grandchildren and a great granddaughter. He exercises every day and is grateful for his health. He has coffee with his wife, well with a photo of her, each morning. She passed away six years ago. Still, they have their morning chat.

Today, after calling one of his kids to plan the next holiday, he is off to doubles tennis, and will use his agility to circumvent some of the hopeful "ladies" and one gentleman who want to date him. Frankie is grateful for the sun, for the air, for the kids that come to learn a little bit about tennis from him and his buddies. The tennis buddies love volunteering to teach the kids and Frankie particularly enjoys praising them for their efforts. He likes to see the sunlight on their faces and to be of service to the younger generations. In fact, to make the kids laugh, when he gets to the court, he is often seen doing one cartwheel...

Frankie is a "full circle" type of person which means that throughout his life, he has felt connected to those around him. A paramedic, he spent years tending to emergency situations and literally touched thousands of lives. He gave so much both professionally and personally. He knew that the people in need relied on his team to help stabilize them and their loved ones both physically and emotionally.

A life well lived; his heart is full. His legacy continues amongst the tennis court kids and his grandchildren who know to send "love, prayers and light" out to the world whenever they hear emergency sirens.

Here's to you Frankie!

————————-

The excerpts do not depict any one person and are derived from an amalgamation of many human nature stories intuited by this author. What stories are missing from this collection of examples that you would like to see included?

Blessings of love and light to all the streams of life force energies touched upon herein. Shine the light so we may learn through the dark times and maintain gratitude. Eventually dark and light are one.

It is not for us to judge whether a person, place or thing is worthy of another person's gratitude. It is the willingness to find an authentic expression of gratitude that is important.

Gratitude lives between the lines of our individual and collective stories. It is not a trophy of good fortune but rather an essential metronome of the heart's Lub Dub. By cultivating gratitude, we ensure strength of heart for the human experience.

Chapter 7
Peacefully on Purpose

Considerations for the ALL

With grateful hearts, peace starts with us. As we weave more forgiveness and gratitude into the microcosm of each of us, we are taking care-filled responsibility for the macrocosm. Imagine that the Earth has its own positive microcosm comprised of all the ways humans did better as they knew better. After we focus on healing ourselves, we gather and turn our healing attention to the world.

We invite historians, scientists, and educated professionals who know the intimate details of what the Earth and her people have endured, to share the Earth's story along the Peace on Purpose Time Circle. I believe we would eventually sense a gratitude reality for the Earth itself. Together, we offer the apologies and forgiveness the Earth deserves from what we historically have done to ourselves, each other and to our planet.

Accessing our true "humane" nature, we can do even better and be even better to the Earth, the animals, oceans, mountains, plants and resources. To the balance of all living systems on Earth. This intention requires the attention of as many of us as possible, so we start acting on our "humane" nature!

We can visualize the healing that may be born from the Earth's perspective if various nations were represented in stating forgiveness, bringing healing to the Earth; witnessed by all people. Further, we may see that the healing of the microcosm of the Earth extends to the Earth's macrocosm which to me is the Milky Way Galaxy and perhaps beyond to include the Universe.

With intention, we include the Universe. Let's join to plant these healing seeds of potential. Together we are "Intention" farmers because peace starts with us. And first, it must start with each of us, individually, so that we can then band together for the greater good. As more of us band together for the greater good other people may hear the call more loudly resounding in their hearts.

How to be is our choice in each moment. **Look at all of us! How can WE be of service to us and to the Earth? To the Universe? Imagine the Peace on Purpose journey of a country, working in harmony with other countries!**

When I had the honor of working at Wolf Connection, we rescued many canines of high wolf content that found their forever homes in good sized habitats of one or more canines depending on compatibility. The animals did not all get along because they were rescued and not a "true" pack as wolves are in the wild. Despite all the "reasons" for disconnection, they howled harmoniously as ONE pack.

They were connected and communicated as a pack entity to alert the team of something awry, for example. They recalibrated their "song" after an animal passed away and the musical note of that animal's individual howl was missing from the choir. Individually, when a new rescue arrived at Wolf Connection, they joined the pack howl at some point, harmonizing their solo into the chorus.

I reflected this pack awareness to guests and program participants. Surely as humanely centered humans we too can "howl" as ONE pack! We too can choose to join the voice of humanity. Peace on purpose is possible and becomes probable once we each join the voice of humane humanity.

After we step across the Bridge of Curiosity and before we enter the theater that has the marquee highlighting our earthly names, we stand and PAUSE. We look beyond to the world theater with "Earth and All" on the marquee banner. Here, with a hand on our heart, we look out as an audience member of planet Earth. We bow our heads in deference to the Light of the highest good of all concerned. We remember that we are audience members of the "All", the Universe as well.

Despite the sense that the problems on Earth are insurmountable we are grateful that the verdant promise of fertilizing Peace on Purpose is worth our efforts. Taking a deep breath, we feel the rise and fall of our chest connecting us to the beat of gratitude; we are doing better as we know better. There is a Lub Dub of Oneness externally and internally if we choose to experience it and share it.

Considerations for Us Moving Forward

Now that we have read through some Time Circle journeys and have seeded some of our own, let's review considerations for moving forward. I have basic ideas for us to create our own daily practice, to assess our perspective and to identify potential culprits that lead us down the path of reaction and judgement, ultimately creating separation until we take the steps to transform the blame. Daily practice also supports us in identifying and embracing gratitude and cultivating self-awareness.

I am certain that you have noticed that this manuscript repeats information! It was written to support us in anchoring in the messages so that in turn we may use the information as we authentically and intuitively continue on our journey remembering that growth is a process.

The intention of the Time Circle is to provide a well-trodden pathway for honest poignancy and forgiveness. We all carry some amount of baggage in life for which we are ultimately responsible. When we are traveling publicly and passing through TSA, we are asked if we packed our own bags and are familiar with its contents. We may have been carrying the bags for years and possibly may have forgotten the contents! The point of the Peace on Purpose journey is to become familiar with what we are carrying, which usually involves blaming others or self.

What's in our bags? We remove the contents and journey to Reclaim, Reframe, Reconcile and Realign with grateful hearts, to the best of our abilities. We are traveling through life and may be asked at certain life stage checkpoints: *Did you pack your own bags?* If we deny responsibility for the contents, we may be thwarted from reaching the intended destination.

As adults with healthy agency, how can we move forward in life if we do not take responsibility? Sure, we can lie about it and fool ourselves for a short time. Eventually, the bags may be too heavy to lift or just produce some drag to our momentum.

Did you pack your own bags? Do you know what is in your bags? This concept causes me to chuckle when passing through security when I am traveling. Knowing what is in our bags, how it got there and what we did to transform it breeds gratitude.

Quick Daily Check-In:

At this point of the journey, we know it is important, with life's busy schedule, to set time aside to mindfully check in with self. Here is what is proposed to us. A daily check-in is suggested to promote increased self-awareness and gratitude. We decide what time of day we do it to create consistency. Daily check-in should be mindful and brief.

If we have a permanent Time Circle, we can easily walk the circle, intuitively stop and then wonder as to the significance of why we stopped at a certain section. Without setting up a Time Circle on the ground, we can draw a small circle on paper, for example, and demarcate the four cardinal points. Using a sand garden provides an important sensory experience to do a quick hand sized circle check in.

We look at, or call to mind, photos of ourselves that correspond to each life stage as we travel around the Time Circle so we can connect more deeply. We discover gratitude for each stage of either our lives or a new endeavor.

After exploring the Time Circle, we take notice if there is need to set aside a later time to circle a bit longer. We are honest and ask for assistance from a friend or professional as needed. As an action step we send out a simple message expressing gratitude for someone in our lives. We are also invited to send a message to self as well.

Monthly Check-In List to Consider

About once a month or bimonthly, we review the list to create Gratitude awareness with respect to the cardinal points.

What's going on with me is ...

The story I am telling is ...

I blame this person or circumstance ...

Has anyone truly had malicious intentions?

After I spew judgements about how others are wrong or whether I am wrong, what's at risk if I am wrong? I am afraid to admit _______ to myself.

My statements of Forgiveness are ...

I am noticing that my body is feeling ...

I am noticing that my emotions are ...

I am noticing that my self-talk is saying ...

Because the truth is ...

The Truth is ...

And the Truth IS ...

My inner/outer agreements are ...

Is there more? Am I complete? Do I require extra assistance?

My Gratitude Reality is ...

Points to Assist Developing an Authentic Practice

As we move through the process, we are aware that some of us lead with our mind, emotion or body. It is important to develop the check in process that is intuitive for each of us!

Writing For Emotion Access

Some of us may like to write or draw to connect with our emotions. Along with the Time Circle journey, we are encouraged to keep a daily journal if that resonates with us. To help us get started dialoguing with aspects of ourselves we can look at Lucia Capacchione's *The Power of Your Other Hand.*

Using the method presented may be a good first step for some of us to connect with self through journaling after which we can use the information to give voice in the Now along the Time Circle to anchor the healing experience into our being.

Capacchione's method allows us to write or draw as ourselves in the Now using our dominant hand. We write a letter to a younger aspect of self, for example, using our dominant hand and have the aspect of self respond to us via writing with the non-dominant hand. It is a powerful way "in" for those of us who may need a written warm up to speaking around the Time Circle. Check out *The Power of Your Other Hand* for further insights.

We can identify and write about the Time Circle journey and review concepts that we are exploring and learning.

"Considerations" for the Journey Check In

We pause and identify at least one "Consideration" that expanded our awareness from the day before or at the end of the day. This could become a ritual meditative or verbal contemplation on the way to or from a daily travel routine.

- Bridge of Curiosity
- I Am RIGHT
- Assessment versus Judgement
- Own the Connection
- The Choice to Do Better
- We Are All Growing at Various Rates
- The Crazy Mix of Life! Soul's Curriculum
- Healing Like Peeling Layers of an Onion
- Story Telling
- Mourning to Morning Milestones
- Gratitude Reality

As a result, if identifying the expanded awareness:

What new thoughts have we "scripted"?

What new emotions are emerging, blanketed by gratitude?

How are we feeling in our bodies? Has there been a release of tension that warrants more stretch with loving application and breath?

Body Check In

If we lead with our bodies, activating the core through position, intention and breath can help us to further assimilate the wisdom we glean from the Time Circle practice and anchor it into our body. Our body may guide us to where we are storing emotion from the past. We use correct breathing to improve posture and to be present in the Now. I highly recommend "Deep Core Activation" by Rodolfo Mari to incorporate a deeper body and breath connection as we rescript and renew. (Request a copy at MysticBodyworks.com)

Construct Challenge for Feeling Stuck!

Sometimes we may feel a little stuck! Mental constructs dictate the beliefs we hold about ourselves and how we relate to others. Sometimes the beliefs we have held dear or consistently can block us from moving forward. If this happens, it is okay because we know that we are vibing to the rhythm of sacred timing. When I know that I am struggling with a process, I pause and take a break. To challenge myself during the "time off" I may do something silly, inviting myself to be more open to seeing things in a different way.

For example, I might take a vase and instead of filling it with water and flowers, turn it upside down and use it as a pedestal for a small object. I may take my lunch plate, turn it over and put my sandwich and chips on the underside. Very silly, right? Over time I begin to question the meaning of "upside down" so that when it feels like things are going "wrong" or are "upside down" in my life, I know I can challenge myself to pause before I make a negative final conclusion. I may see negatively for some time and then I can turn things around like the pedestal that is now ready to receive water and cut flowers.

I do this because it makes me laugh and opens me to using what I already know in new ways. The experience reminds me that I can discover other ways of thinking and being by rearranging my "routine" thoughts and actions. I can be more open to view the puzzle pieces of my life from above.

<u>We Are Ready</u>

As we approach the Time Circle, we first step onto the Bridge of Curiosity. Do we have any bags we want to leave behind to signal our intention to release baggage we may be carrying? Remember, it is okay to proceed whether we leave bags behind or carry the bags because we know we can always step back and pick them up once more or drop them whenever we wish.

From the center of the bridge, when we see our name in huge letters alighted on the marquee in the near distance, we note how we are feeling in our body, mind and heart. Perhaps we are feeling anxious, angry, or sad. Maybe our body is tense with shallow breathing. Perhaps we are simply heartbroken or bursting with joy and excitement!

We pause and take time to listen within and notice how we are doing. We take a deep breath, filling ourselves with awareness and acknowledgement of our efforts. We step forward because we know how to do this!

We spend time looking through our Time Circle of life photos and simply just be with our memories, forgiveness and hearts, inviting healing into the NOW. Our relationship with ourselves is precious and deserves support. We are open to explore the depths of gratitude.

We are ready!

We step towards the theater with our name in huge, alighted letters! We especially want a good seat in the theater of our life so we can hear every spoken line, notice body language, and gain more awareness and insight when reviewing ourselves.

We are invited to sit amongst the "audience", to observe ourselves on the stage of life.

Seated, we review the Playbill which displays our names. We are the "stars" of the show!

***Playbill* PEACE ON PURPOSE JOURNEY**

CAST:

- Past, Present & Future Self
- Loved ones & Friends
- Blame
- My Story in Sacred Timing
- Forgiveness & Gratitude

SPECIAL GUESTS: Light Beings & Guides

ENSEMBLE: Considerations for the Journey

ACT I:

- East- New Beginnings (birth & childhood); South- Discovery (adolescence)
- West- Responsibility. Harvest of Self (adulthood); North- Wisdom & the Generative Elder

ACT II:

- Reclaim – Reframe – Reconcile - Realign

FINALE: Gratitude Reality metronome of our heart's Lub Dub strength for this human experience.

We sit comfortably in our seats. We take a few deep cleansing breaths, settling in with grateful hearts as we observe the stage of our lives. We recognize the players: the many aspects of self courageously circling the life stages. Each step, a beat of honesty comprising the rhythm of our human experience.

We feel poignant with heartfelt compassion as we witness how we choose to be in each moment, doing better as we know better, embracing the "mistakes" as learning opportunities.

Gratitude Reality gets a standing ovation as we cheer, sometimes with tears streaming down our cheeks.

We cheer for ourselves! It feels a bit foreign to some of us, and we persist. Little by little, it is feeling more natural to cheer for self.

We PAUSE the show of our life now and then.

We stand up, take a breath and look all around us with a perspective of gratitude.

We see Light Being Ancestors and Guides seated in the audience, amongst all our memories, thoughts, Time Circle photos and future interactions awaiting their turn on stage.

We hear applause beyond our own efforts, and we realize that the Light Being Ancestors and Guides are cheering us on through every separation and connection. We know that they are lovingly holding for our learning – in our sacred timing – transforming blaming into Being.

We look at the stage of our lives through the lens of "humane centering."

We know that the Ancestors and Guides are grateful for our efforts. And their applause? It replenishes our souls with acceptance and echoes the gratitude metronome of our hearts' Lub Dub strength for this human experience.

We allow the encore. We breathe it in. There is always more. We got this!

Why do we walk the Peace on Purpose journey? We persevere because we know what we want. We want to do better as we know better. We want the fertilized Truth. We want the congruent Monet of our Soul. We want Peace on Purpose for ourselves, each other, the Earth and beyond.

How to be. It is our choice at every moment.

Finding Peace on Purpose in sacred timing is our true "humane" nature.

Onward!

Final Gratitude Dedications

My paternal grandmother for planting seeds of Being and Belonging in me and trusting me to continue sowing Life's meaning with Fierce Love.

To first loves, the memories of which remind me that I am a creative, loving and lovable being. I became my own first love too. It is never too late.

To Myriam Guerci, Ancestral friend and relentless warrior. I am in awe of and so grateful for your loving loyalty and perseverance. I will admit it here, in this dedication... Perhaps I am more stubborn than you! Thank you for holding on, for letting go and for being my friend. (Explore EarthInspiredSpirit.com for sacred native jewelry and other products.)

Brianna McGrath, who reached out in her magical way and invited me back onto life's joyful journey, complete with a pack of pets! Her sparkling light guided me home to the east coast, into the Mystic, so to speak, where a depth of my earthly self belongs. I am ever grateful for the welcoming and generous support of her family as well.

Elizabeth Parascandola Clee who role modeled good strong leadership to me since I was nine years old and through a lifelong friendship of love, wisdom, laughter and steadfast companionship that no amount of distance could deter.

To Kristine LaVigna - Wise and trusted friend since I was age fifteen, who when visiting me in California in 2018 gave me an unequivocal response to my question: "Run for your life" she advised. I listened.

Paula Mitchell - Inspirational leader and brilliant friend who is a force at directing authentic power. Thank you for always sharing your Light with me. As the Director of LA Innocence Project, she guides her team to exonerate the wrongly convicted exposing systemic and human flaws in the criminal justice system. This is Peace on Purpose in action. (innocencela.org)

Jennifer Thompson, a radiant being whose friendship, coaching, positivity and co-creational fun guide my heart and writing. Remember to check out *Martyrs, Victims & Jerks (nomvj.com)*

To my ex-husband for blending his family and extended family of Carol Berry and the Kabellis' with mine and embarking on a journey that brought learning opportunities for personal growth. When I look at our children, I see so much love and I know we did well.

Cate Salansky, who taught me that I can align for the Light of the greater good no matter what. How I value the lessons we shared, and the long wolf path we walked.

To dear ones who took the time to read the manuscript and offer invaluable feedback! Especially the brave ones who read a few different versions! Deep gratitude! Rachel Ferretti, Kris LaVigna, Ethna Flaherty, Paula Mitchell, Myriam Guerci, Elizabeth Parascandola Clee, Lisa Spigai, Jackie Spigai and Kellie Lussier. Thank you to Ronnie Costanza, Gina Raiano, Maureen O'Hanlon Freder, Jennifer Thompson, Valerie Fresh, Annemarie Seifert, Julie Avila and Tim Quinn. Your time and willingness are so appreciated.

Creative graphic forces of Kat Wright, Christian LaVigna and Bella D'Amico for their patience with me and combining intuition with their talents in creating the Peace on Purpose design. Bravi!

Craig Junjulas, spiritual teacher in my college years who instructed me to only "trust" teachers who taught me to identify and follow my own wisdom. (higherselfdiscovery.com)

Sr. Kathleen Deignan Ph.D., cherished mentor, Catholic nun and theology professor at Iona University, who back in 1986 advised that the potential demise for humans may be the result of the imbalance between technology and spirituality. How we grow is so important. (earthandspiritcenter.org)

To Kate, who served the lockdown days of Covid with me reminding me what day it was, who with her big heart, nurtured a me that was somewhat lost in transition.

Sky, the archangel Russian Blue cat, panther of my soul.

D'Marcel Napier, whose reflected strength inspired me to go to battle for myself, reminding me that she has my back.

Sophie Clerico, whose light reflects a similar path. We will never retire from Light work!

To Cindy Starry, for reminding me to include reverence for the Land in all considerations. See the Earth Toy for more inspiration from Cindy in revering the Land (livingart.io)

Karla Wehbe, dear friend who first asked me to speak to my inner five-year-old back in 1991.

To Roth Herrlinger and Rich Thomas, dearest friends who coached and held me at times, through the years, when I felt the feminine in me collapse.

Rich Thomas, dear friend and Sound Editor extraordinaire, for patient assistance with the challenge of the audio book and for lovingly sharing the "May I Suggest" song by Susan Werner.

Woman Within Int'l (WomanWithin.org) and other retreat organizations of similar vibration, for assisting the willing with the journey of forgiveness and personal responsibility.

Ozzy, shaman wolf who had a comical disposition and yet immense fortitude beneath the surface. I invite in this way of being.

I am so grateful for the good work of Wolf Connection in transforming and empowering program participants and guests. Donating to good causes and/or volunteering, is good medicine! Some other good works organizations I was blessed to know during my time at Wolf Connection (WolfConnection.org) are listed below and include all organizations of similar vibration:

> To the Topa Institute (formally known as Ojai Foundation), and Center for Council for reflecting and providing an ancient healing and council practice in today's world. (Topa.Institute) (CenterForCouncil.org)

> Street Poets Inc., for sharing the truth of important stories and reminding us to cultivate human connection through word melodies that pulse colorful sound waves for all people. (StreetPoetsInc.com)

> Heart Math, for inviting people to raise awareness and synchronize and balance the lub dub of humanity. Thank you, Erin Toppenberg, for sharing Heart Math with me! (HeartMath.com)

To ARC (Anti-Recidivism Coalition), for their incredible efforts in supporting the reentry of the formally incarcerated. (AntiRecidivism.org)

Youth Mentoring Connection for cultivating communion in community by inviting "at-risk" youth to cultivate connection to self and other with primal awareness. I believe we are all at risk of not having enough primal connection. (YouthMentoring.org)

To Dr. Greg Vanvakaris, beloved chiropractor and healer in Los Angeles, who simply asked me out of the blue: "Can you see yourself doing something else one day?" and pierced a veil, for a future transition I had not yet known I would require or want. Thank you for asking! (@thehealthspotstudiocity)

Human Garage and orgs of similar vibe for bringing harmonious awareness to the important legacy of fascia releasing and balancing of the human body. (HumanGarage.net)

Mystic Massage team (mysticmassagect.com), Dr. Stephen Choman (ponoacupuncture.com), Dr. Stacy Oliveira DPT (ohspt.com) and Ron Agostini PT of Mystic (PTofMystic.com) for holistic healing practice especially in my time of need.

Rodolfo Mari of Mystic Bodyworks (Mysticbodyworks.com) for sharing his patience, intuition, humor and skillful presence in assisting me on this last leg (pun intended) of me stretching to fully inhabit this body of mine, connected to my breath of life. I am arriving, rediscovering my soul family.

Ted Riter, Life Coach, for holding sacred space so I could hear my wisdom. Joyful gratitude! (TedRiter.com)

Apex Protection Project, and other organizations of similar vibe for the heart of their rescue work and offering of some free education sessions for youth as a reflection of their passion for posterity. (ApexProtectionProject.org)

I'm grateful to beloved friends, those present and passed on, especially those with whom I share wolf stories. You have all touched my heart and encouraged me to change and grow for the better.

Gratitude to Pat Dobie MFA of lucidedit.com. I appreciate your skill and intuition with the content edit. I know you want to edit this again because I made changes ☺ I will be in touch!

To the nearly five-year-old, in a store amongst the very scary Halloween life size decorations, when I was in the process of a major life transition and full of anxiety, who provided me with the gift of reflection. You are the Light on the path of Courage.

To all the wolves in my bones: your melodic howls free the souls of all who were immobilized and Now Flow with Grace. *Viva Luce*. And so, it is.

To my newest great nephew: teach us to fly and to serve humanity. Show us how we look from the perspective of the stars.

To posterity and lineage – How can WE be of service to the greater good?

========

To me,

Sail on silver girl...

Your time has come to shine

All your dreams are on their way...

(Simon & Garfunkel "Bridge Over Troubled Water")

As you sail, the winds strip you of all that does not serve the highest good. Some personas may be ripped from you while others fly easily away with purpose like the veil of a bride on the run.

Relax, allow and breathe in the transformation. As you continue to arrive the winds will further clear and reveal the paths of service.

Follow the path illuminated and know well the source of its glow.

Love, ME

And remember, there is always more.

Onward!

=======

Dedicated to all Seekers of the Find Peace on Purpose Journey

"May I Suggest" Song & Lyrics by Susan Werner

May I suggest. May I suggest to you

May I suggest this is the best part of your life

May I suggest

This time is blessed for you

This time is blessed and shining almost blinding bright

Just turn your head

And you'll begin to see

The thousand reasons that were just beyond your sight

The reasons why

Why I suggest to you

Why I suggest this is the best part of your life

There is a world

That's been addressed to you

Addressed to you, intended only for your eyes

A secret world

Like a treasure chest to you

Of private scenes and brilliant dreams that mesmerize

A lover's trusting smile

A tiny baby's hands

The million stars that fill the turning sky at night

Oh I suggest

Oh I suggest to you

Oh I suggest this is the best part of your life

There is a hope

That's been expressed in you

The hope of seven generations, maybe more

And this is the faith

That they invest in you

It's that you'll do one better than was done before

Inside you know

Inside you understand

Inside you know what's yours to finally set right

And I suggest

And I suggest to you

And I suggest this is the best part of your life

This is a song

Comes from the west to you

Comes from the west, comes from the slowly setting sun

With a request

With a request of you

To see how very short the endless days will run

And when they're gone

And when the dark descends

Oh we'd give anything for one more hour of light

And I suggest this is the best part of your life

===

Song and lyrics by Susan Werner

Check out the beautiful song online!

(SusanWerner.com)

Be connected and explore services and products. We will continue to grow together.

PEACE

Only through compassion and inner peace can one spread peace in the world. Inner peace leads to a peaceful individual and then this peaceful individual can build a peaceful family, then a peaceful community, then a peaceful world.

by H.H. The XIVth Dalai Lama

Thank you for joining me on the Peace on Purpose Time Circle Journey.

Many Blessings to you!

About the Author

Giulia Cappelli has a master's degree in counseling psychology with an emphasis in Spiritual Psychology from the University of Santa Monica (UniversityofSantaMonica.edu). She shares the Peace on Purpose journey and methodology to inspire self and others to find greater inner peace with the understanding that healing one's inner world will translate to healing the world.

In as much as Peace on Purpose is a culmination of years of teachings gleaned from education, personal growth and coaching, this manuscript also marks a beginning whereby we may work to raise the vibration of life on planet Earth. Together, let's be Intention farmers and plant healing seeds of potential that grow in sacred timing, watered by our willingness, for the highest good of all concerned.

Read more at https://findpeaceonpurpose.com.